101 great
science
experiments

101 great science experiments

Neil Ardley

DK PUBLISHING, INC.

LONDON, NEW YORK, MUNICH,
MELBOURNE and DELHI

Project Editor: Jenny Vaughan
Art Editor: Nigel Hazle
U.S. Editor: Alison Weir
Managing Editor: Helen Parker
Managing Art Editor: Peter Bailey
Production: Samantha Larmour
Picture Librarian: Lucy Pringle

First published in the United States
in 1993. This edition published in
the United States in 2006 by
Dorling Kindersley, Inc.,
375 Hudson Street,
New York, New York 10014

A catalog record for this book is available from
the Library of Congress

ISBN-13: 9-780-75661-918-3
12 13 14 15 16 17 18 19 20
025-KB500-Nov/1993
Printed and bound by Toppan, China

Discover more at
www.dk.com

Be a safe scientist

Always follow all the steps in each experiment carefully.

Take care, especially when handling hot or heavy objects, glass, scissors, knives, matches, candles, and batteries.

Do not smell things, put them in your ears or mouth, or close to your eyes unless the book tells you to do so.

Do not play with electric switches, plugs, outlets, or electrical machines.

Make sure you clean up after each experiment.

👫 This sign in a step means that **extra care** is needed. You must ask an adult to help you with it.

CONTENTS

AIR AND GASES

WATER AND LIQUIDS

HOT AND COLD

LIGHT

AIR AND GASES

Air is all around you – but you are hardly ever aware of it. You cannot see it, and you only feel it in a strong wind. But you breathe air all the time. It keeps you alive – and animals and plants too. Air is needed to burn fuel and to make many machines work. Aircraft use it when they fly. Air is made up of "gases" – substances that can change shape and "expand" or grow bigger to fill any shape or space.

Air support

A bicycle pump forces more and more air into the inner tube of a tire. The air pushes out on the walls of the tube. It pushes so hard that it can support the weight of both the bicycle and the rider.

Buoyant balloons

These balloons contain helium, which is a very light gas. Balloons filled with helium float in air.

Nitrogen

Oxygen

Carbon dioxide and other gases

Argon

Big let down

As a parachute falls, air pushes upward against it, so it drops slowly and safely to the ground. Air is made up of two main gases, called nitrogen and oxygen, with small amounts of other gases.

Big breath

When you breathe in, air enters your lungs. You can find out how much air your lungs can hold by taking a deep breath and then blowing through a tube into an upturned jar of water. The air from your lungs pushes water out of the jar.

1 Crush with air

Make a plastic bottle collapse without touching it! The air does the job for you. You cannot feel air, but it presses against every surface. This is called "air pressure."

You will need:

Ice

Funnel

Hot and cold water

Plastic soft drink bottle

Bowl

1 Stand the bottle upright in a bowl. Pour the hot water into it and leave it for a short time.

2 Screw the top on the bottle. Lay the bottle in the bowl and pour ice and cold water over it. Then stand it up.

3 The bottle collapses! As the warm air inside the bottle cools, it exerts less pressure. The pressure of the air outside is stronger and crushes the bottle.

---

2 Seal with air

Keep water from falling out of an upturned glass. A card can stick to a glass and keep the water in it, as if by magic! Air pressure forces the card upward, against the glass. The pressure is strong enough to stop the weight of the water pushing the card away.

You will need:

Thin flat card

Glass

Water

1 Hold the glass over a sink or a basin. Carefully pour some water into the glass.

The rim must have no chips in it.

2 Place the card on the glass. Hold it down so the card touches the rim all the way around.

3 Still holding the card, turn the glass upside down. Let go of the card. The water stays in the glass!

3 Weigh some air

When something is very light, people often say "It's as light as air." But air is not light at all. Do this simple experiment to show that air is really quite heavy.

You will need:

Balloon pump

Two balloons

Rubber band

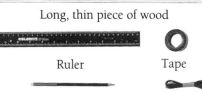
Long, thin piece of wood

Ruler

Tape

Pencil

Thread

Two tacks

1 Use the ruler to find the center of the wood. Then mark it.

2 👫 Push a tack into each side at the center mark.

3 Tie the thread to the middle of the rubber band.

Attach the neck of the balloon to the far end of the wood.

If the wood does not balance, attach modeling clay to the higher end.

4 Fix the loops of the rubber band around the tacks. Lift the wood by the thread. It should balance.

5 Tape one of the balloons to one end of the wood.

6 Tape the second balloon to the other end of the wood. Check that it still balances. Then remove one balloon and blow it up.

Move one of the balloons if the wood does not balance.

When the balloon has been inflated, it becomes heavier because it contains air.

The empty balloon has no air in it, so it is lighter than the inflated one.

7 Tie the neck of the blown-up balloon and attach it to the wood in the same place as before. The balloon makes the wood lose its balance.

Drinking with a straw
When you drink through a straw, the weight of the air helps you. The air above the drink pushes on the surface of the liquid. As you suck, it forces the liquid up through the straw to your mouth.

4 Discover the gases in the air

Put out a candle without blowing on it or touching it. When you do this experiment, you show that air is a mixture of invisible gases. One of these is especially important. It is oxygen, which is used when things burn and produce energy.

You will need:

Candle

Colored water

Glass jar

Bowl and candle holder

1 Put the candle in the holder and place it in the bowl. Then pour in the water.

2 👥 Ask an adult to light the candle. Then place the jar over it. Leave it for a little while.

The flame uses up oxygen gas in the jar.

The water rises up to replace the oxygen. The remaining gas in the jar is mainly nitrogen.

3 At first, the water level in the jar rises, and then the flame suddenly goes out!

Air and energy
Like other cars, this racing car gets its energy from petrol burning in its engine. Burning fuel provides most of the energy we use for heating and powering machines. This process uses oxygen, which comes from the air around us.

5 Form a gas

Inflate a balloon without blowing into it or using a pump! You can do this by making a gas and then getting it to go into a balloon. The gas is called carbon dioxide. It is this gas that forms the bubbles in soda water and carbonated drinks.

You will need:

Vinegar

Sodium bicarbonate

Balloon

Funnel

Narrow-necked bottle

1 Pour some vinegar into the narrow-necked bottle until it is about a quarter full.

2 Using the funnel, fill the balloon with sodium bicarbonate powder.

3 Stretch the neck of the balloon over the neck of the bottle.

Do not let the sodium bicarbonate escape from the balloon.

Exploding drink
Shake a bottle of soda, then unscrew the cap. The drink fizzes up out of the bottle! Carbon dioxide gas is dissolved in the water in the drink. It is kept under pressure in the bottle. When you unscrew the cap, you reduce the pressure and the gas bubbles escape up out of the water.

4 Lift the balloon so that the sodium bicarbonate falls into the bottle. The vinegar begins to fizz and the balloon slowly starts to inflate.

As more gas forms, its pressure increases and the balloon expands.

The vinegar reacts with the sodium bicarbonate to release bubbles of carbon dioxide gas.

6 Make a volcano erupt

Build a model volcano – then make it erupt! You can make "red-hot lava" flow down the sides. Although the lava is not real, your model volcano works like a real one.

You will need:

Vinegar

Small plastic bottle

Sodium bicarbonate

Large dish or tray

Funnel

Red food coloring

Sand and gravel

1 Add red food coloring to the vinegar. This makes your "lava" red, like the real red-hot lava in a volcano.

2 Using the funnel, half fill the bottle with sodium bicarbonate. Then stand the bottle upright in the middle of the dish.

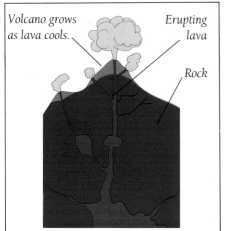

Volcano grows as lava cools.

Erupting lava

Rock

3 Pile gravel, then sand around the bottle to make the volcano. Quickly pour some red vinegar into the bottle and watch the volcano erupt!

Bubbles of carbon dioxide gas form in the bottle and force out the red vinegar.

Exploding mountain
A long pipe leads down from the top of a volcano to a deep underground chamber. There is melted rock in the chamber and very hot gases. The pressure of the gases sometimes forces the molten rock up the pipe to the surface. The red-hot melted rock, called "lava," erupts from the volcano and flows down its sides. There it cools and becomes solid. Eruptions cause the lava to build up and the volcano grows taller.

7 Make a wing fly

When birds and aircraft fly, moving air around their wings helps carry them high into the sky. Build and fly a model wing. It shows how moving air lifts up a wing and keeps it airborne.

You will need:

Short length of thread

Drinking straw

Tape

Sharp pencil

 Hairdryer

Scissors

 Light, stiff paper

1 Fold the paper in two. Make one side of the fold a little smaller than the other.

2 Turn the paper over. Tape the edges together to make a wing shape.

3 Use the pencil to make two holes in the wing, one above the other.

4 ⚕ Cut a piece of drinking straw, long enough to go through the holes.

5 Push the straw through the holes. Attach it firmly with tape.

6 Feed the thread through the straw and tie it to something sturdy.

7 ⚕ Blow air on the wing, which rises up on the thread. It's amazing!

Use the hairdryer to blow air over the curved top of the wing.

As the air passes over the wing, it speeds up.

As the air moves faster, its pressure falls.

Still air under the wing has a higher pressure. It pushes the wing upward.

Blow them apart?
Tape cotton threads to two table-tennis balls and hang them about 6 in (15 cm) apart. Try blowing air between the balls. Instead of separating them, the moving air draws them together. As air moves, its pressure falls. The balls move toward the lower pressure, so they swing together.

8 Detect moisture in the air

Although air does not feel wet, it contains moisture. Moisture in the air is called "humidity." The humidity of the air is constantly changing, as this experiment shows.

You will need:

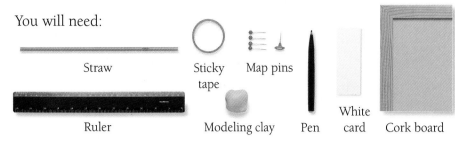

Straw · Sticky tape · Map pins · Ruler · Modeling clay · Pen · White card · Cork board

1 👫 Draw a scale on the white card, marking it at one-sixteenth of an inch (2 mm) intervals. Pin the card to the cork board.

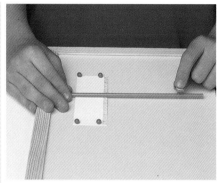

2 👫 Push a pin through a straw close to one end. Pin the straw to the board, so that the long end points to the middle of the scale.

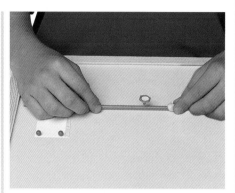

3 Press some modeling clay into the short end of the straw. Use just enough clay to balance the straw when the board is upright.

4 Get a friend to pull a hair carefully from your head – tell them not to pull too hard, or it will hurt!

Hair absorbs and loses moisture easily.

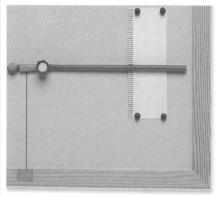

5 Tape one end of the hair to the short end of the straw and the other to the board's frame. Stand the board upright.

Weather house
This model house can tell you what the weather is going to be like. The man comes out if the air is moist. This means rain is likely. If the air is dry, the woman comes out. When she appears, this shows that there is dry weather ahead.

6 In dry air, the hair shrinks and pulls the straw up the scale. In moist air, the hair expands and the straw falls down the scale.

9 Measure the wind

You can feel the wind – but can you tell where it is coming from? It is important to know because a change in the wind can affect the weather. Make a wind vane to determine the wind's direction.

You will need:

Long tack

Modeling clay

Scissors

Plastic pot

Ruler

Glue stick

Drinking straw and pencil with eraser

Thin, colored card

1 Use the pencil to make a hole in the middle of the pot. Then push the sharp end of the pencil through the hole.

Make sure the pot holds the pencil firmly.

2 Cut out four small triangles and two large ones from the colored card.

First mark the triangles on the card with a ruler and pencil.

3 Glue each of the four small triangles to the plastic pot. Look at the picture to see where they should go.

The triangles point outward in four directions.

4 Cut short slits in both ends of the straw. Insert the two large triangles into the straw to make an arrow-shaped pointer. This is called a "vane."

Push the pointed end of one triangle into the straw to make the wind vane's tail.

Push the base of the other triangle into the straw to make the vane's pointer.

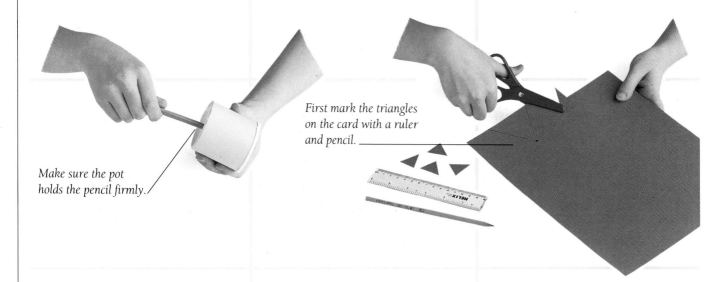

5 Carefully push the tack all the way through the center of the straw. Then push it into the eraser on the pencil end.

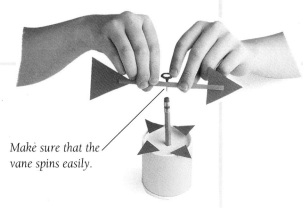

Make sure that the vane spins easily.

6 Make a ring of modeling clay and push the pot firmly into it, so it cannot blow away. Your wind vane is ready to use.

Press the pot firmly into the modeling clay.

The modeling clay holds the wind vane steady.

Whirling in the wind

As well as finding out the direction of the wind, it is also important to measure the speed of the wind. High-speed winds may cause damage and they may be dangerous to ships and aircraft. This instrument is called an anemometer. It measures the speed of the wind. The moving air makes the cups whirl around and the wind speed shows on the scale. There is a scale to describe wind strength. It ranges from 0 (calm) to 12 (a hurricane).

The wind spins the cups.

The wind speed is shown on the dial.

7 Place your wind vane outside. The vane swings around in the direction of the wind.

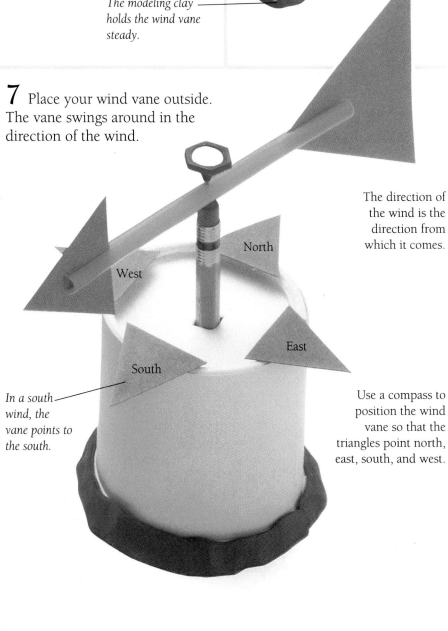

North

West

East

South

In a south wind, the vane points to the south.

The direction of the wind is the direction from which it comes.

Use a compass to position the wind vane so that the triangles point north, east, south, and west.

WATER AND LIQUIDS

Water is wonderful. You can have fun swimming and playing in water. Rain is not so much fun, but we could not live without it. It brings us the water we need to drink and to grow crops for food. Water is a "liquid," which is a substance that flows easily. There are many other liquids. Oil, such as cooking oil, is another. When liquids are cooled, they turn to solids. Water freezes to become hard ice. Heating water turns it into a gas called "water vapor," which disappears into the air. When water vapor cools, it turns back to liquid water.

Building with water
A snowman is made with solid water! Snowflakes consist of ice. They are made up of ice crystals which form in clouds in cold weather.

Water for life
People, animals, and plants all need water to live. Water helps keep your body working, so that you stay alive.

World of water
This photograph of the Earth shows the blue oceans and the white clouds that bring rain. Most of the brown land with no clouds is a huge desert where no rain falls.

The power of water
Water can change the shape of the land. Waves battering the shore wear away the rocks. Rain washes soil into rivers, which carry it away.

Mostly water
There is as much water in these buckets as in this girl's body! More than half of your body is water.

10 Make things sink, then float!

A huge ship floats on water, even though it is very heavy. Yet a small, light object such as a marble sinks! The weight of the objects does not matter. Whether or not something floats depends on how much water it "displaces," or pushes aside.

You will need:

Modeling clay

Marbles

Glass tank or bowl of water

1 Drop marbles into the water. They quickly sink to the bottom. Roll the clay into a ball.

The displaced water pushes on the objects, but not enough to make them float.

2 The clay ball also sinks. Like the marbles, it does not displace much water.

3 Remove the marbles and the clay ball. Shape the clay to make a boat.

More water has been displaced. It pushes with more force and can support the clay boat, making it float.

4 Now the clay floats! The boat is bigger than the ball was and displaces more water.

The extra displaced water supports the weight of the marbles.

5 Add a cargo of marbles. The boat settles lower, but displaces more water and still floats.

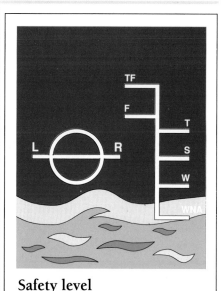

Safety level
An overloaded ship settles too low in the water and could sink. Marks on a ship's side show safe loading levels.

11 Find out about floating

An object floats in water if it displaces enough water. But how much water is "enough?" Find out by collecting the displaced water and weighing it. It always weighs the same as the floating object.

You will need:

Kitchen scale

Pitcher of water

Big glass jar

Small glass jar

Large dish

Fill the jar to the brim.

1 Remove the pan from the scales and re-set the scale to zero. Put the scale in the dish. Rest the big jar on the scale and fill it with water. Note its weight.

2 Float the small jar in the big jar. It displaces water, which spills out into the dish. The weight of the big jar does not change.

3 Carefully remove the big jar and the scale from the dish. Put the pan on the scale and adjust them to zero. Pour in the water that had spilled into the dish.

4 Write down the weight of the water in the pan. Remove the pan and re-set the scale to zero.

Afloat like a boat
When you float in water, your body displaces water, like any other floating object. The displaced water weighs as much as you do. It pushes up against your body and supports it so you do not sink.

5 Now weigh the small jar that was floating in the big jar. You can see that it has the same weight as the water it displaced.

12 Command a deep-sea diver

At your command, a toy diver will dive into a bottle of water and then return to the surface. The diver you make works in the same way as submarines and other vessels that can dive deep under the sea.

You will need:

Plastic pen top

Modeling clay

Glass of water

Thin clear plastic bottle

If there is a hole in the tip, seal it with clay.

1 Make your toy diver by sticking a small piece of modeling clay to the pen top.

Only the tip should be above the water.

2 Put the diver in a glass of water. Add or remove clay until it only just floats.

A bubble of air is trapped inside the pen top. This makes it float.

3 Fill the bottle to the top with water. Put the diver in and screw the top on tightly.

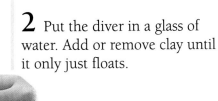

4 Squeeze the sides of the bottle. The diver sinks to the bottom!

Water enters the pen top. The bubble gets smaller, and no longer supports the pen top.

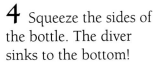

Water leaves the pen top. The air bubble gets bigger again and makes the pen top float once more.

5 Release your grip on the bottle. Now the diver rises back to the top.

Down in the depths
This underwater vessel explores the ocean depths. It has tanks that are flooded with water to make it dive. To make it rise to the surface again, air is pumped into these tanks. This drives out the water, and the vessel floats.

13 Make an underwater volcano

Did you know that you can get water to float on water? Hot water always rises to the surface and floats on cold water underneath it. Show this happening by making a "volcano" erupt under water and send up a huge plume of "smoke."

You will need:

Scissors

Paintbrush

Narrow-necked
small bottle

Hot and
cold water

Red food
coloring

String

Large
glass jar

1 ✂ Cut a long piece of string. Tie one end firmly around the neck of the small bottle.

2 Tie the other end of the piece of string around the neck of the same bottle to make a loop.

3 Pour cold water into the large glass jar until it is about three-quarters full.

4 ✂ Fill the small bottle with hot water. Add food coloring to turn the water bright red.

5 Hold the bottle by the loop of string. Lower it gently into the jar of cold water.

6 The hot red water rises from the bottle like smoke from an erupting volcano.

Hot-water holes

There are deep holes in the ocean floor. Water, heated by the hot rocks deep in the Earth's crust, shoots out of these holes and rises to the surface of the sea. Divers have discovered strange sea creatures that live around these hot-water holes.

14 See how liquids float and sink

Liquids can float and sink just as solid objects can. It all depends on something called "density." A substance with a lower density weighs less than the same volume of one with a higher density. An object or liquid will float only in a liquid more dense than itself.

You will need:

 Colored water

 Syrup

 Vegetable oil

Large container

Selection of objects to float

1 Carefully pour syrup into the container until it is a quarter full. It is easier if you pour the syrup over the back of a spoon.

2 Slowly pour the same amount of vegetable oil into the container. Then add the same amount of colored water.

3 The three liquids separate into three layers and float on each other. Now add the objects you plan to float.

4 The objects float at different levels. They sink until they reach a liquid of a higher density than themselves. They float on that liquid.

Water is more dense than the oil but less dense than the syrup.

The grape is more dense than the water but less dense than the syrup.

Liquid tester
A lump of modeling clay on a straw makes a "hydrometer," which measures density. The level at which it floats depends on a liquid's density. The denser the liquid, the higher it floats.

15 Find out if liquids mix

It is easy to color some liquids, but not others. See how oil "resists" being tinted with food coloring. This means it does not let the coloring mix into it, and the color cannot spread through oil. Then find out what happens to the color in water.

You will need:

 Food coloring

 Glass beaker

 Spoon
Dropper

 Cooking oil

1 Pour some water into the beaker. Then add some cooking oil. You can see how they form two separate layers because oil and water do not mix.

2 Carefully add a few drops of food coloring to the beaker. Use a dropper if necessary. The drops float around in the oil.

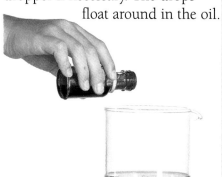

3 Using a spoon, push the drops of food coloring into the water. The color bursts out as the drops meet the water and mix with it.

16 Test the flow of liquids

It takes much longer to pour syrup into a glass than to pour water. This is because the syrup has a high "viscosity." This means it does not flow easily. Test the viscosities of different liquids. The ones in this experiment should be easy to find at home.

You will need:

Liquids such as water, cooking oil, clear liquid soap, syrup, and vinegar

Small jars and marbles

1 Fill the jars with different liquids. Drop a marble into each one.

2 The slower the marble falls, the higher the viscosity of the liquid.

17 Grow a stalactite

Stalactites are long, thin columns of minerals hanging from the ceilings of caves. They form over many centuries as water drips and deposits its minerals. But *you* can grow one in less than a week!

You will need:

Short length of yarn   Paper clips   Pitcher of warm water   Dish   Spoon   Two jars   Baking soda

1 Fill both jars with warm water. Add baking soda and stir until no more dissolves.

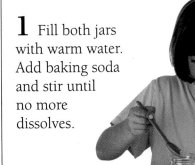

2 Attach paper clips to the ends of the yarn. Place the ends in the jars, so that the wool hangs between the jars.

Baking soda solution

The soda solution flows along the yarn.

Baking soda solution

3 Place a plate between the jars to catch the drips. Leave the jars for several days. A white stalactite grows down from the yarn. A stalagmite grows up from the plate.

Drip of soda solution

More crystals form in dish.

The stalactite grows as each drip evaporates and leaves a little soda behind.

Stalactites
Water flowing underground dissolves minerals as it seeps through rocks. It then deposits the minerals as stalactites when it drips through a cave roof. Water falling from the end of a stalactite builds up a column of minerals on the floor called a stalagmite. The stalactite and stalagmite may eventually meet to form a pillar.

18 Measure the rain

Rain falls from the clouds, which contain millions of tiny water droplets. These come together, forming raindrops that fall to the ground. Make a simple rain gauge to measure rainfall. This is the amount of rain that falls over a certain time.

You will need:

Ruler and marker

Measuring cup

Small, clear bottle

Large, clear plastic bottle

Scissors

1 Cut off the tops of both bottles, using the scissors. Make sure that the edges are straight.

2 Fill the cup a quarter full. Pour the water into the small bottle. Mark the level.

3 Repeat step 2 several times, so that you have a series of marks on the side of the bottle.

4 Empty the small bottle. Place it inside the large bottle. Put the top of the large bottle upside down over the small bottle. It forms a funnel.

Empty the bottle after measuring the rainfall. Put it back in the same place.

5 Stand the bottles outside on a table or a wall to catch the rain. Record the water level in the small bottle each morning. This is the daily rainfall.

Chart showing the rainfall for twelve months

Weather station
Each day, scientists called meteorologists take detailed measurements to help them keep track of the weather and forecast how it will change. They record the amount of rainfall, the highest and lowest temperatures, the humidity, the speed and direction of the wind, and the air pressure.

6 Add up the rainfall for each week or each month. Then make a chart to show how much rain falls over several weeks, months, or even a whole year.

19 Is water hard?

Water can be "hard," but not hard like rock. If tap water is hard, it contains a lot of dissolved minerals. Soap does not easily form bubbles in hard water. Do this experiment with soap to find out if the water from your faucets is hard.

You will need:

Tap water   Two screw-top jars   Small open jar   Distilled water   Liquid soap

Spoon   Dropper

1 Mix liquid soap with some distilled water in the small jar. Distilled water is not hard.

2 Pour distilled water into one screw-top jar, and the same amount of tap water into the other.

3 Put a drop of liquid soap solution into the jar of tap water. Screw on the lid.

4 Shake the jar. If it does not foam, repeat step 3 and shake it again. Count how many drops you need to make the water foam.

If the tap water needs more drops to make it foam than the distilled water, it is hard.

5 Repeat steps 3 and 4 with the distilled water. Did the tap water need more drops to make it foam?

Water softening
Hard water builds up scaly mineral deposits in kettles and pipes. It can be softened by passing it through a filter that uses chemicals to remove the minerals from the water.

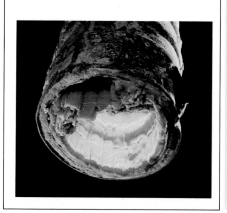

20 Race a speedboat

Make a paper boat race across a bowl – just by touching the surface of the water! This happens because there is a force present, called "surface tension."

You will need:

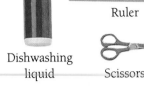

Pencil

Ruler

Dishwashing liquid

Scissors

Large, clean plastic bowl of water

Colored card

1 Draw the shape of your boat on the card. This one has a triangular shape.

2 Carefully cut out your boat shape. Place it on the water and let it float.

3 Squeeze a small drop of the dishwashing liquid on your finger.

4 Dip your finger in the water, just behind the boat. The boat shoots forward across the bowl.

The dishwashing liquid weakens the surface tension behind the boat.

Make metal float
Gently place a paper clip on the water's surface, and it will float! The surface tension of the water is strong enough to support very light objects, such as paper clips.

The surface tension is stronger in front of the boat. This pulls the boat forward.

You must change the water in the bowl if you want to try again.

21 See plants drinking

Plants need water to live, just as you do. By making some flowers change color, you can see how plants absorb water. It flows through a plant's stem and into its leaves and flowers.

You will need:

Four glasses

Different colored inks or food coloring

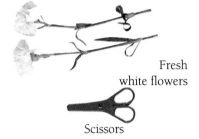
Fresh white flowers

Scissors

1 Pour a little food coloring or ink into each glass. Then add some water.

2 👫 Trim the stems of the flowers. Split part of the stem of one flower in two.

3 Put a flower in each glass of colored water. The split stem goes in two glasses.

4 Leave the flowers in a warm room. Very slowly, they change color.

Green flower

Red flower

Red water travels up the stem to the petals, staining them red.

Each part of the split stem feeds different colored water into the flower.

Thirsty leaves

Place a twig with leaves on it in a glass of water. Add some cooking oil, and make some marks on the glass. Observe this for a few days to see how the level of the water falls as the leaves suck up the water. The layer of oil on the water keeps it from evaporating, so you can be sure that all the water has been absorbed by the plant.

5 Each half of the flower with the split stem turns a different color. One half of the split stem feeds red water into it and the other half feeds blue water.

Red and green flower

HOT AND COLD

Something that is hot, like a hot drink, feels very different from something cold, like ice cream. But both sensations are caused by the same thing: heat. The difference is that cold objects contain less heat than hot ones. Our bodies make heat from our food. We also get heat from the Sun and from burning fuels.

How hot?
A thermometer measures the "temperature," which is how hot or cold something is. Temperature is measured in units called "degrees." This thermometer is showing a temperature of 26.2 degrees.

Fire and flames
Heating some materials makes them catch fire. This has happened to the trees in this forest. The flames of the fire produce heat, so more material starts to burn and the fire spreads.

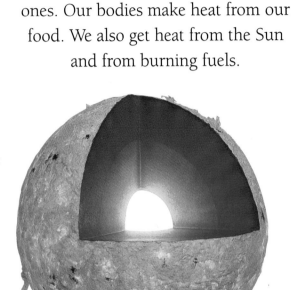

A ball of fire
The Sun is a huge ball of very hot gas. It glows with light and creates vast amounts of heat in the form of invisible heat rays. These travel through space and warm the Earth.

Keeping cool
You wear thin clothes in hot weather. These allow heat to escape from your body, so you do not get too hot.

Staying warm
You wear thick clothes in cold weather. These keep you warm because they keep heat from escaping your body.

22 Build a simple thermometer

A thermometer usually has a thin tube of colored liquid in it. This liquid moves up and down inside the tube, which is marked with a scale showing degrees. The level of the liquid in the tube indicates the temperature.

You will need:

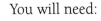 Modeling clay

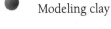 Clear straw

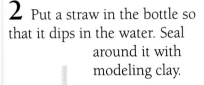 Card Scissors Cold water Food coloring Colored markers Glass bottle

1 Pour cold water into the bottle until it is about three-quarters full. Add a few drops of food coloring.

2 Put a straw in the bottle so that it dips in the water. Seal around it with modeling clay.

The seal must be airtight.

3 Blow gently into the straw. The water rises up it. Stop when it is halfway up.

The black mark shows a normal temperature.

4 Cut two slits in the card. Slide it over the straw. Make a black mark to show the level of the water.

The red mark shows a high (warm) temperature.

Heat makes the air inside the bottle expand and push the water up the straw.

5 Put the thermometer in a warm place. The water rises. Mark the level in red.

The blue mark shows a low (cool) temperature.

The air inside the bottle contracts as it cools, sucking the water back down the straw.

6 Put the thermometer in a refrigerator for a while. The water level falls. Mark it in blue.

23 Race some beads

Heat spreads better through some materials than others. Show how well some common materials "conduct" (spread) heat through them. Good conductors take in most heat.

You will need:

Glass beaker

Beads

Butter or margarine

Wooden spoon

Drinking straw

Metal spoon

Plastic spoon

1 Use butter to stick one bead to each of the spoons and to the straw. Stand them in the beaker.

2 Pour in hot water. Heat moves up the spoons and straw and melts the butter. The bead that falls first was stuck to the best conductor.

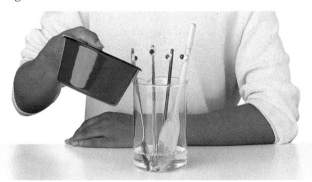

24 Circulate some heat

Show how heat moves around a liquid. This movement is called "convection." It happens in air, too. When you put a heater in a room, its heat spreads by convection.

You will need:

Heatproof glass dish

Dropper

Candle

Wooden blocks

Food coloring

Cooking oil

1 Put the candle between the blocks. Ask an adult to light the candle.

3 Warm currents circulate in the oil. They carry drops of food coloring with them.

The oil at the surface cools and sinks back to the bottom.

2 Pour cooking oil into the dish and place it on the blocks. Put drops of food coloring at the bottom.

As the oil gets hotter, it rises.

Balls of food coloring

25 Keep a drink cool

When a liquid evaporates and changes into a gas, it takes in heat from its surroundings. Refrigerators use this principle to keep things cool. Try making your own refrigerator.

You will need:

Two drink cans   Glass dish   Cup of water   Flowerpot   Plant spray gun

This can will warm up in the Sun's rays.   *This can will stay cool during the experiment.*

1 Do this experiment on a sunny day. Take two drink cans. Place one in the sunshine, and the other in a glass dish.

2 Cover the can in the dish with a flowerpot. Pour cold water over the flowerpot until it is fully soaked.

3 Leave the flowerpot to stand in the Sun's rays. Spray it with water now and again to prevent it from drying out.

As the water evaporates from the wet flowerpot, it takes heat from inside the flowerpot. This draws heat from the can and keeps the drink cool.

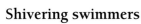

4 After about an hour, take both cans and taste the drink from each one.

5 You will notice that the drink from the can that has been exposed to the Sun is the warmest. The wet flowerpot acts like a refrigerator and keeps the other drink cool.

Shivering swimmers
It is quite common to shiver soon after emerging from the ocean or a pool, even if the weather is not particularly cold. As the water evaporates from your wet skin and suit, it draws heat from your body, making you feel cold. It is good to have a towel ready to wrap yourself in!

26 Store some heat

Hot drinks lose heat easily, so they soon cool down. Make a heat store and keep some warm water in it. The store helps stop heat from escaping, so the water inside it stays warmer for much longer.

You will need:

Tape

Wide cork

Big jar with lid

Small jar with lid

Small glass

Warm water

Aluminum foil

Scissors

1 Wrap two layers of foil tightly around the small jar, with the shiny sides facing in. Fasten the foil with tape.

The shiny foil helps keep heat in the small jar.

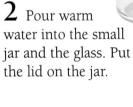

2 Pour warm water into the small jar and the glass. Put the lid on the jar.

The lids stop the heat from escaping upward.

3 Place the cork in the bottom of the big jar and stand the small jar on it. Put the lid on the big jar.

Heat does not pass easily through the cork and the air in the large jar.

Heat leaves the sides and top of the glass.

Water in the glass loses heat more quickly than in the small jar.

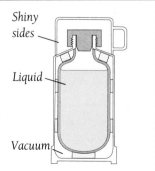

The water in the small jar stays warmer for longer.

Heat barrier
A thermos flask keeps drinks hot or cold. It has two containers with tight lids, like your heat store. The inner container has shiny sides and a double wall with a "vacuum," or empty space, inside. It is so difficult for heat to leave or enter the flask that its contents stay hot, or remain cold, for a long time.

Shiny sides

Liquid

Vacuum

4 After ten minutes, take the small jar out. The water in it is still warm, but the water in the glass has cooled.

27 Fight a fire

Light a candle – and then put out the flame, as if by magic! This can be done because things burn only if they get oxygen from the air. Take away the supply of oxygen, and the fire goes out.

You will need:

Spoon

Sodium bicarbonate

Matches Candle Vinegar Glass dish Modeling clay

1 Using the modeling clay, stick the candle to the bottom of the dish.

2 Sprinkle some sodium bicarbonate around the candle.

The top of the candle must be lower than the top of the dish.

3 👫Ask an adult to light the candle with a match.

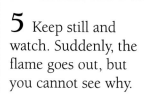

4 Add some vinegar. The sodium bicarbonate begins to froth.

As the candle burns, it takes in oxygen from the air.

5 Keep still and watch. Suddenly, the flame goes out, but you cannot see why.

Invisible carbon dioxide fills the glass and covers the flame. It cuts off the oxygen supply.

The froth must not reach the flame.

The vinegar and the sodium bicarbonate release bubbles of carbon dioxide gas.

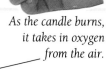

The match goes out as it enters the carbon dioxide.

Battling the flames

Fire fighters cover a fire with a layer of water, foam, or carbon dioxide. This layer stops air from reaching the flames. To go on burning, the fire needs oxygen from the air. Without oxygen, the fire goes out.

6 👫Try to light the candle again. It's impossible!

28 Slice some ice

Cut right through an ice cube – and leave it in one piece! You do not use a knife for this amazing trick. You just cut the ice with a piece of wire.

You will need:

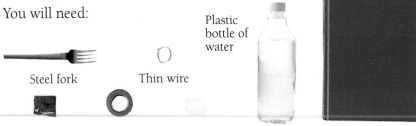

Steel fork   Thin wire   Plastic bottle of water

Aluminum foil   Tape   Ice cube   Heavy book

1 Tape the fork to the table edge. Put the book on the handle.

Make sure the fork cannot move.

2 Make a loop of wire and fix it securely to the bottle.

Knot the ends of the wire tightly together.

3 Place the ice cube on a square of foil on the fork.

4 Loop the wire over the ice cube. The weight of the bottle pulls the wire into the ice.

The wire pulls so hard that its pressure makes the ice beneath it melt.

When the pressure from the wire has gone, the water freezes again.

5 Slowly, the wire cuts right through the ice cube.

Speed on the ice
Skaters can move quickly over ice. Their weight causes a film of water to form just beneath the blades of their skates. The skates slide easily along on this slippery film.

6 Pick up the cube after the wire has passed right through it. The cube is still all in one piece!

29 Make your own ice cream

Make some tasty ice cream and find out how to make things freeze without putting them in the freezer. This is an old-fashioned way of making ice cream. It still works well.

You will need:

Cream

Ice cubes

Dish towel

Chocolate milk powder

Tablespoon

Salt

Glass

Large bowl

Milk

1 Mix one spoon of chocolate, two spoons of milk, and one spoon of cream in the glass.

2 Put some ice cubes in the bowl and sprinkle a lot of salt over them.

3 Place the glass of ice cream mixture in the large bowl, on top of the salted ice cubes.

4 Build up more layers of ice cubes and salt around the glass.

When salt is mixed with ice, it makes the ice melt. It also makes it colder.

5 Place the dish towel over the bowl. Leave the ice cream mixture to set for an hour. Stir it every few minutes.

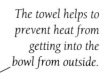

The ice needs heat to melt. It takes this from the ice cream mixture, which gets so cold that it freezes.

The towel helps to prevent heat from getting into the bowl from outside.

Spikes of ice
Icicles form where water drips over the edge of a cold surface. The cold surface draws heat from the water, which turns to ice. An icicle begins to form. As more water runs down the ice and freezes, the icicle grows.

6 Take the glass out of the bowl, and taste your homemade chocolate ice cream.

LIGHT

Light makes it possible for you to see the world around you. Sources of light, such as the Sun and light bulbs, produce light rays. These bounce off objects, such as this book. The rays then enter your eyes, and you see the objects. We use light to form "images" or pictures of things.

Broken and bent?
The pen standing in this glass of water is in fact straight. It looks strange because water bends the light rays coming from the pen to your eyes.

Too small to be seen?
You can see very tiny objects or creatures with a microscope. The image you see is highly "magnified," or much bigger than the actual object or creature.

Mirror images
You can see images of things in mirrors. The curved mirrors at the front and back form large and small images.

Quick as a flash
This camera makes a bright flash to give enough light to take a photograph. The light travels from the camera to the girl in two billionths of a second.

36

30 Play with shadows

Scare your friends by casting some spooky shadows on the wall! This will also show you how light travels in straight lines. Shadows form when an object blocks the light.

You will need:

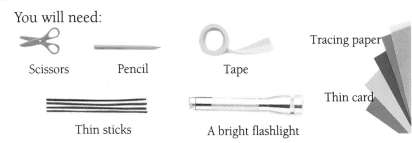

Scissors   Pencil   Tape   Tracing paper

Thin sticks   A bright flashlight   Thin card

1 Trace patterns of ghosts from a book, or invent some of your own and make drawings of them.

2 Transfer your ghost patterns from the tracing paper to the pieces of thin card.

3 👥 Carefully cut out the ghost patterns and tape each one to the end of a stick.

4 Hold the patterns near the wall. Shine a flashlight on them, and large shadows of the ghosts appear on the wall!

A dark shadow appears on the wall.

Rays of light come from the flashlight and light up the wall.

The shadow forms where the rays are blocked by card and cannot reach the wall. The shadow has the same shape as the card because the rays of light are straight and cannot bend around the edges of the card.

Sunny time
You can tell the time with a sundial. The Sun casts a shadow of a tilted bar onto a set of lines, which mark the hours. Throughout the day, the shadow moves as the Sun travels across the sky. The position of the shadow on the lines gives the time.

31 Look around corners

Build a periscope. You can use it to see over walls or people's heads and to peep around corners. A periscope works by using mirrors to reflect rays of light.

You will need:

Make these two sides the same length.

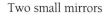

Triangular card

Two small mirrors

Scissors

Tall, empty carton

Pen

1 Use the triangular card to help you draw two diagonal lines on one side of the carton.

2 Carefully cut a slot along each line. The slots should be just wide enough for the mirrors to fit into.

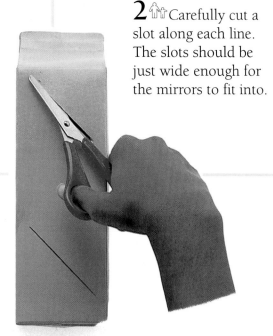

3 Draw and cut two more slots on the other side of the carton.

These slots must be directly opposite the first slots.

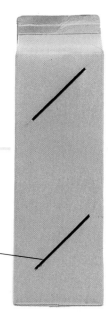

4 Carefully push the mirrors into the slots. They should fit snugly, so that they cannot slide out of the carton.

The shiny side of the top mirror faces downward.

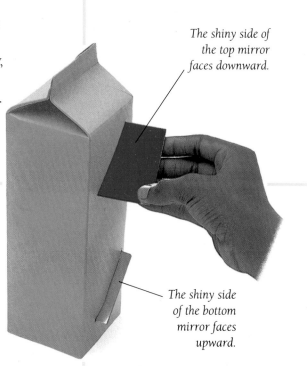

The shiny side of the bottom mirror faces upward.

38

5 👫 Draw a large square at the top of the carton in front of the mirror. Carefully cut it out.

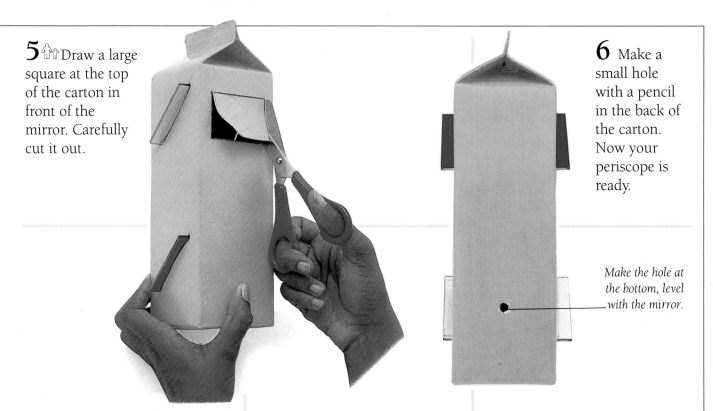

6 Make a small hole with a pencil in the back of the carton. Now your periscope is ready.

Make the hole at the bottom, level with the mirror.

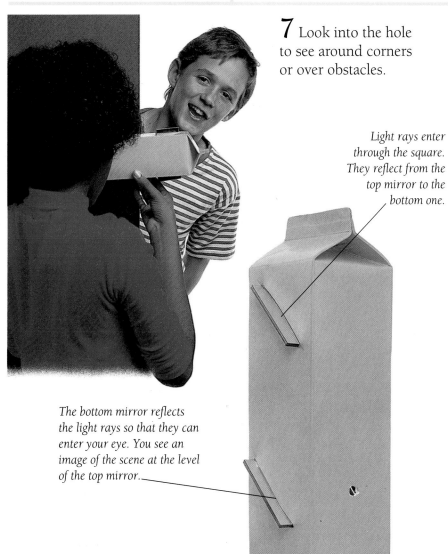

7 Look into the hole to see around corners or over obstacles.

Light rays enter through the square. They reflect from the top mirror to the bottom one.

The bottom mirror reflects the light rays so that they can enter your eye. You see an image of the scene at the level of the top mirror.

What's up there?

When a submarine is under water, the crew may want to see above the waves. They may need to find out if there are any ships nearby. They raise a periscope to the surface of the water and look around. The periscope has a long tube that reflects light rays from above the surface of the water down to the submarine. A member of the crew looks into it to see what is going on above the submarine. The periscope may then be brought back down again.

39

32 Build a kaleidoscope

Use mirrors and beads to make a colorful kaleidoscope. All you have to do is shake it, and beautiful patterns form, one after another.

You will need:

Sharp pencil

Flashlight

Tape

Beads

Scissors

Card and tracing paper

Three small mirrors

1 Tape the three mirrors together to form a triangle.

The shiny sides go inside.

2 Draw around the mirrors on the card.

3 👥 Cut out the triangle. Use a pencil to make a hole in the middle of it.

4 Tape the triangle to one end of the mirrors.

5 Stretch the tracing paper over the other end of the mirrors. Tape it firmly in place.

6 Drop some beads through the hole. Your kaleidoscope is now ready.

7 Shine the flashlight onto the tracing paper and look through the hole, into the kaleidoscope. You see several images of the beads combined, forming a pattern. Shake the kaleidoscope to change the pattern.

The mirrors reflect light from the beads to form several images of them.

You, you, you, you, you ...
You can see many images in two parallel mirrors. This is because they keep reflecting light rays between them.

33 See double

Use water to turn one button into two! This trick depends on the way light rays bend as they enter and leave water and glass. This bending of rays of light is called "refraction." Refraction also makes a straight ruler look bent when it is standing in water.

You will need:

Glass   Pitcher of water   Button

1 Put the button into the glass. Try to get it to lie right in the middle of the glass.

2 Gently pour some water into the glass until it is half full.

The button must not float.

3 Look down at the glass from one side. It looks as if there are two buttons in the glass!

Two sets of bending light rays from the button reach your eyes, so you see it twice.

34 Make your own flashlight

We need light to drive out darkness – and we use electricity to make that light. Without electricity, we would have no safe light in our homes or streets. You can carry your own source of light with you if you have a flashlight. Press the switch, and a beam of light cuts through the darkness. Batteries in the flashlight provide the electricity it needs.

You will need:

 Two 1.5V batteries

 Two paper fasteners

Sharp pencil
Screwdriver

 Aluminum foil

Paper clip

Bulb in holder

Cotton

Scissors

Three pieces of wire with bare ends

Plastic tape

Empty dish-washing bottle

1 Cut off the top of the bottle. Using the pencil, make two small holes in the side, as shown.

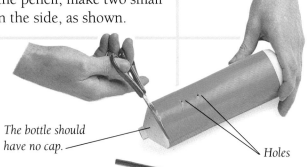

The bottle should have no cap.

Holes

2 Tape foil to the inside of the bottle top. Make sure the shiny side faces outward.

3 Using the screwdriver, attach two of the pieces of wire firmly to the bulb-holder.

Make sure the wires cannot come loose.

4 Tape the batteries together. Then tape the third piece of wire to the lower battery.

Tape the top of one battery to the base of the other.

5 Tape one of the wires from the bulb-holder to the terminal on the top battery.

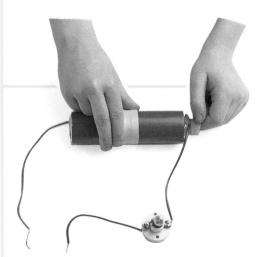

6 Thread the wire from the bottom battery through the lower hole. Pack cotton into the bottle and insert the batteries.

Push cotton around the batteries to hold them firmly in place.

7 Thread the wire from the bulb-holder through the top hole in the bottle. Attach both wires to paper fasteners, then push in the fasteners.

8 Place the bulb-holder on the batteries and tape the center of the bottle top over the bulb.

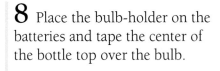

9 Bend the paper clip and fit one end under the lower paper fastener. This is the switch.

Closing the switch lets electricity flow from the batteries along the wires to the bulb.

Bright bulb

Inside an electric bulb, there is a thin wire called a "filament." This glows white-hot when electricity flows through it. Gas inside the bulb helps stop the filament from burning away while it is so hot.

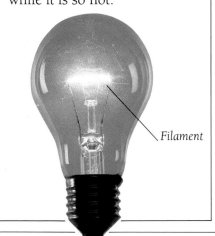

Filament

10 Press the other end of the paper clip against the top fastener. The flashlight lights up!

The bulb lights up as electricity flows through it.

The light reflects from the shiny foil to produce a bright beam of light.

35 Make a slide projector

Slide shows and movies are a lot of fun, but you do not need complicated equipment to project pictures. Make your own projector with a flashlight and magnifying glass.

You will need:

Rubber band

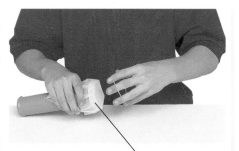
Color slides

Tracing paper

Flashlight

Magnifying glass

1 Place a sheet of tracing paper over the end of a flashlight. Put a rubber band over the tracing paper to keep it in place.

The tracing paper must fit tightly over the flashlight.

Hold the slide upside down. Keep the torch and slide level and in line with each other.

2 Switch on the flashlight and point it at a wall. Hold a color slide in front of the flashlight. Aim the flashlight beam so that the light passes through the slide.

The magnifying glass makes light rays passing through the slide come together on the wall to form an image.

3 Ask a friend to turn out the light. Then get your friend to hold the magnifying glass about 4 in (10 cm) in front of the slide.

Alter the positions of the slide and magnifying glass to get a clearer picture.

4 The picture on the slide should now be visible on the wall. If it is not clear at first, adjust the distance between the slide and the magnifying glass to focus the image.

36 Bend a beam of light

Light travels in straight lines, but its path can be altered by reflecting it off other surfaces. This experiment uses the reflective properties of water to bend the path of a light beam.

You will need:

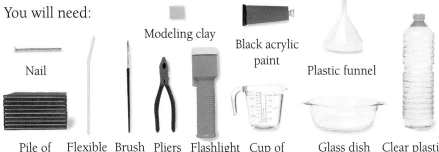

Modeling clay

Black acrylic paint

Plastic funnel

Nail

Pile of books · Flexible straw · Brush · Pliers · Flashlight · Cup of water · Glass dish · Clear plastic bottle

1 Paint one vertical half of the plastic bottle black and let it dry.

2 👥 Ask an adult to make a hole about 2.5 in (6 cm) up from the base on the black side. A hot nail makes a neat, round hole, but it must be held with pliers.

3 Push the end of a flexible straw into the hole. Press modeling clay around the hole to prevent leaks. Plug the end of the straw with modeling clay.

4 Fill the bottle with water. Place it on a pile of books and position a glass dish underneath the straw.

5 Turn out the light. Shine a flashlight at the hole from the bottle's clear side. Remove the plug from the straw and put your finger under the stream of water. You will see a tiny spot of light dancing on your finger!

The sides of the stream of water reflect the light back and forth. This stops the light from escaping and makes the light follow the water's path.

Light messages
Telephone conversations and computer data are often sent along cables as pulses of light. Inside the cables, the light travels along very thin glass threads called optical fibers. The light bounces along the optical fibers as it reflects off the sides of the glass threads.

37 Construct a camera

Build a model of a simple camera to learn how it works. Your model camera uses a magnifying glass to form a picture, just as the lens in a real camera does.

You will need:

Tape

Empty tissue box

Magnifying glass

Tracing paper

Cardboard tube

Pen

Scissors

1 Hold the tube on the side of the box opposite the opening. Draw around it.

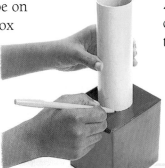

2 Carefully cut out the circle you have drawn on the tissue box.

3 Push the tube into the hole. The tube should move in and out.

4 Tape the magnifying glass firmly to the end of the tube.

5 Tape the tracing paper over the opening in the box. Now you can use your model camera.

Taking photographs

A real camera has a lens like the magnifying glass, and film in place of the tracing paper. When you take a photograph, light passes through the lens and forms an image upside down on the film. The film records this image. When the film is developed, you can see the image on a print or a slide.

6 Point the camera at a bright object. An image of it appears on the tracing paper.

Move the tube in and out until the image is sharp.

The magnifying glass is a lens. It makes the rays of light from the flowers bend and meet on the paper.

An image forms where the rays of light meet. It is back to front and upside down.

38 Create photos with light

Find out how photography works by making a photographic picture. You do not need a camera or any special equipment – just a few objects, such as a comb and a feather. It only takes a few minutes for a picture of these objects to form.

You will need:

Packet of photographic paper

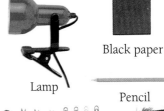
Lamp

Black paper

Scissors

Pencil

Small, flat objects

1 👫 Draw some interesting shapes on the black paper. Then carefully cut them out. The shapes can be anything you want them to be.

Shapes such as moons and stars work well.

2 Take one piece of the photographic paper from the packet. Quickly lay the black paper and objects on it.

Before you get the paper out, make the room as dark as possible.

3 👫 Place the lamp so it points at the paper. Switch it on and leave it on for several minutes. Then switch it off.

Do not disturb the paper and objects.

Photo booth
In a photo booth, a lens forms images of you on a strip of photographic paper. A machine in the booth treats the paper with chemicals to make the pictures form permanently.

4 Remove the objects from the paper. A picture of them has been left behind!

The paper goes dark where the light reaches it.

The parts that were covered stay white.

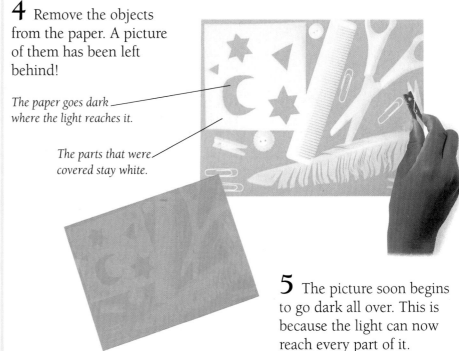

5 The picture soon begins to go dark all over. This is because the light can now reach every part of it.

COLOR

Imagine a world without color. It would be like living in an old black-and-white movie! Color helps bring beauty to our world. There are beautiful colors in nature, and we use color in our clothes and to decorate our homes. Color is in the light that comes from objects. Red light comes from red objects, for example. We detect color when the light enters our eyes.

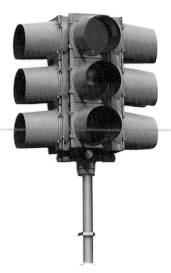

Color codes
We give colors certain meanings. In traffic lights, red means "stop" and green means "go."

Curve of colors
A rainbow occurs when the Sun lights up a shower of rain. The raindrops turn the white sunlight into bands of color. You can only see a rainbow if the Sun is shining behind you.

Colors for camouflage
Some animals, such as this green chameleon, have colors that match their surroundings. This makes it hard for other animals to spot them.

Colorful creatures
Many animals, such as these beautiful butterflies, have bright colors. These colors may attract other animals or warn off enemies.

39 Make a rainbow

You can see a rainbow without having to wait for rain. "White" or colorless light is in fact a mixture of all colors of the rainbow. Water can split this light into these colors.

You will need:

Modeling clay

Mirror   Jar of water   Bright flashlight   Shallow dish   White card

1 Pour water into the shallow dish until it is about half full.

2 Put the mirror in the dish. Use modeling clay to fix it so that it slopes.

3 Shine the flashlight on the part of the mirror that is under the water.

As the white light from the flashlight enters and leaves the water, it splits up into bands of color.

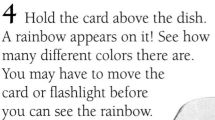

4 Hold the card above the dish. A rainbow appears on it! See how many different colors there are. You may have to move the card or flashlight before you can see the rainbow.

The mirror reflects the light from the flashlight so that it strikes the card.

Inside a rainbow
When you see a rainbow, you are seeing rays of light from the Sun. These rays of white light have been reflected by the drops of rain, which makes them split up into all the colors of the rainbow.

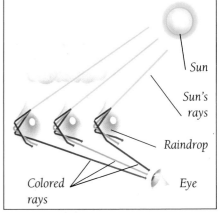

Sun

Sun's rays

Raindrop

Colored rays   *Eye*

40 See a sunset

The Sun often turns a lovely orange or red when it sets at dusk. Find out why this happens by making your own sunset. You can do this using a flashlight and a glass of milky water.

You will need:

Milk

Glass beaker of water

Flashlight

Spoon

1 Shine the flashlight through the beaker of water. It looks white, like the Sun when it is high up in the sky.

2 Pour a little milk into the water in the beaker.

3 Stir the water gently, so that it all turns slightly white.

4 Shine the flashlight through the water again. Now the light looks orange-red, just like the setting Sun!

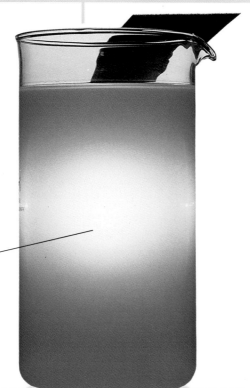

Particles of milk in the water cut out some of the colors in the light coming from the flashlight. Only orange and red rays get through.

Rosy dawn and fiery dusk
When the Sun is low in the sky, in the morning and evening, its light passes through more air than at other times of day. Tiny particles in the air stop much of the Sun's light. Only orange and red light gets through.

41 Discover hidden colors

Paper that can soak up water can separate colors from ink or food coloring. This is because it soaks up some colors faster than others. Find the hidden colors in dark liquids!

You will need:

Dropper

Paper clips

Colored inks and food coloring

Blotting paper

Small jars

Narrow rod

1 In each jar, make a different mixture of inks and food coloring.

The liquids turn dark as the colors mix together.

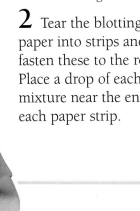

2 Tear the blotting paper into strips and fasten these to the rod. Place a drop of each mixture near the end of each paper strip.

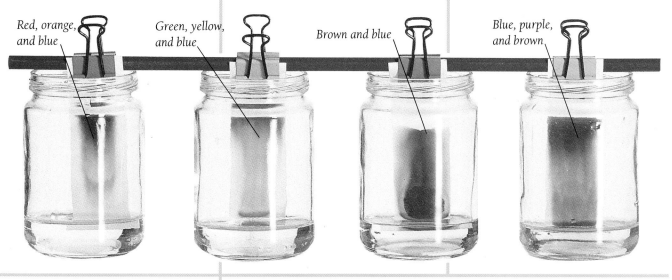

Red, orange, and blue

Green, yellow, and blue

Brown and blue

Blue, purple, and brown

3 Clean out the jars, then pour a little clear water into each one. Lower the paper strips into the jars so that the ends just touch the water. The colors on each strip move up and separate out into different colored bands.

Making paints
A pot of colored paint contains more than one color; the colors are hidden. Paints are made by mixing several different "pigments" or coloring materials together. Different mixtures give different shades.

42 Mix colors together

Pictures in books like this one can show all the colors of the rainbow. Yet only three colors and black are used to make them all. Show how you can mix two or three colors to make any color you want.

You will need:

Scissors

Clear blue, yellow, and red plastic sheets

1 ⚭ Cut the plastic sheets into several strips, all the same width.

2 Place yellow and blue strips on a white surface. Green appears where they overlap and the colors mix.

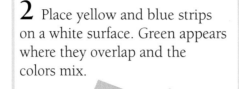

3 Add a red strip to begin a pattern of squares. See how red and yellow mix to form orange.

Orange square

4 Add another red strip to cross over the blue. Purple forms where the two colors mix.

Purple square

5 Add more strips. Red, blue and yellow mix to form several different colors.

Yellow and blue make green.

Yellow and red make orange.

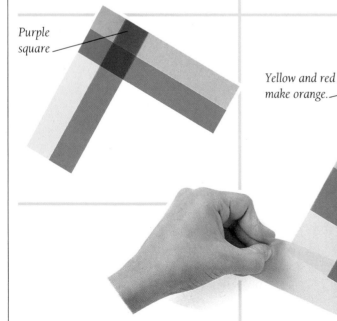

Blue and red make purple.

Bright yellow, red, or blue form where the same colors overlap.

43 Spin some colors

Ordinary white light, such as sunlight, seems to have no color, but it contains all the colors of the rainbow! Color a disk and spin it to show this amazing fact.

You will need:

Violet, indigo, blue, green, yellow, orange, and red paints

Protractor

Paintbrushes

Sharp pencil

Water for paint

1 👥 Cut out a disk of white card. Use the protractor to mark seven sections. Paint each one a different color.

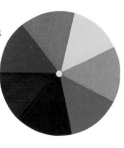

2 👥 Make a hole in the center of the disk. Push in the point of the pencil. Spin the disk. The colors disappear as they mix to form white!

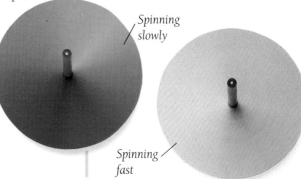

Spinning slowly

Spinning fast

---

44 Change color

An object gets its color by reflecting light. Instead of reflecting all the colors in light, it reflects only some. Show how this happens by using colored cellophane to let only certain colors reach your eyes from an object.

You will need:

Red and green cellophane

Black box with holes in one side and lid

Flashlight

Red playing card

Yellow banana

Green apple

1 Put the objects in the box. Place green cellophane over the hole on the top and shine a flashlight through the side hole.

The red hearts do not reflect green light, so they look black.

Only green light passes through the cellophane.

The yellow banana and green apple both reflect green light.

2 Do the same thing again, this time with red cellophane. The red hearts disappear, while the green apple goes dark. The banana now looks red instead of yellow.

The white card reflects all colors, so now it looks red.

Only red light passes through the cellophane.

The yellow banana reflects red as well as green light.

The green apple does not reflect red light.

Make a liquid change color suddenly, as if by magic! You can use this color change as a test, to find out if a substance is an acid or an alkali – or neither of these.

You will need:

Spoon

Large jar

Distilled or purified water

Sieve

Red cabbage, knife, and chopping board

Saucepan

Four small jars

1 Carefully chop the red cabbage into small pieces.

2 Heat some distilled water in the saucepan. Add the cabbage.

3 Let the cabbage water cool, then strain it into the large jar.

4 Put cabbage water in the small jars and test various substances.

Color varieties

Acids or alkalis in the soil make a difference to the colors of hydrangeas. They have blue flowers if they are growing in acid soil and pink ones if the soil is alkaline.

Lemon juice

Vinegar

Cream of tartar

5 Test lemon juice, vinegar, and cream of tartar. They are acids, which turn the cabbage water red.

Sodium bicarbonate

Tap water

7 Test sodium bicarbonate. It is a weak alkali and turns the cabbage water blue. Tap water may do the same thing.

Distilled water

6 Add distilled water to the cabbage water. It stays reddish purple. The distilled water is neither an acid nor an alkali.

Ammonia

Baking soda

8 Test a little ammonia or baking soda. These strong alkalis turn the cabbage water green.

46 See colors in bubbles

Soap bubbles caught in the light look very colorful. This experiment shows you how to make amazing bubble colors and blow spectacular bubbles at the same time!

You will need:

Glycerol (glycerin)   Dish-washing liquid   Flashlight   Half a liter of water   Plate   Spoon

Straw

1 Stir four spoons of dish-washing liquid (not lemon) and one spoon of glycerol into half a liter of water.

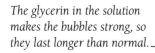
Keep the flashlight beam level with the bubbles.

2 Pour some of the solution on to a plate. Wet the end of a straw and put it in the solution. Gently blow through the other end to create a large bubble.

4 Turn out the light and shine a flashlight at the bubbles. Point the flashlight beam at the "wall" that forms where the two bubbles meet.

3 Carefully remove the straw from the bubble. Blow a second bubble beside the first one. Try to make sure that the bubbles are about the same size.

Light from the torch reflects off both the front and back of the bubble wall. The two reflected beams of light mix, or "interfere," with each other, creating amazing colored stripes.

The glycerin in the solution makes the bubbles strong, so they last longer than normal.

5 View the wall between the bubbles from an angle. Beautiful colored bands appear across the bubble wall! Adjust the position of the flashlight if you cannot see them at first.

47 Print pretty patterns

Print some colorful and pretty patterns on paper. The colors transfer to the paper in the same way that they do when color pictures are printed in books.

You will need:

Palette   Linseed oil   Thick paper   Dish of water   Poster paints   Paintbrush

1 Put some poster paints on the palette.

2 Mix a little linseed oil with each color.

3 Put one color from the palette on the brush and gently add the paint to the water.

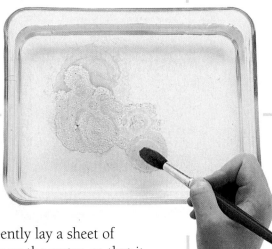

4 Add another color. Swirl the colors to make a pattern.

5 Gently lay a sheet of paper on the water, so that it lies on the surface.

6 Carefully peel the paper away from the water. Lift it out and lay it on a flat surface.

7 Let the paper dry. Try printing more patterns with other colors.

The colored oil does not mix with water, so it transfers to the paper.

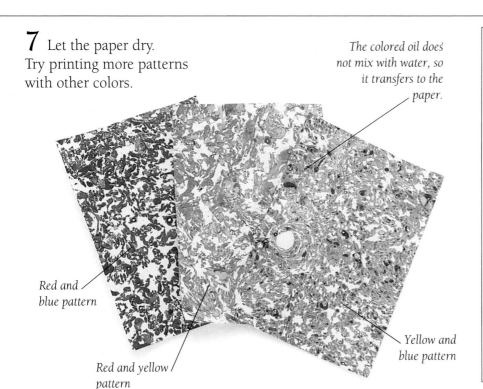

Red and blue pattern

Red and yellow pattern

Yellow and blue pattern

Printing in color
Color printing presses have rollers on which pictures are formed with colored inks. Paper passes through the rollers and the colored ink transfers to the paper, making color pictures.

48 Get colors from nowhere

Make bright colors appear in a clear piece of plastic. This happens if you look through some kinds of sunglasses. The white light coming from the plastic contains all colors. The sunglasses cut out some of these colors while others get through.

You will need:

Polarizing sunglasses

Plastic cassette box

Lamp

1 👭 Place the lamp above the cassette box and switch it on.

2 Put on the sunglasses and look through them at the box.

3 Bright colors appear in the box! The plastic affects the white light coming from the lamp so that only certain colors get through the sunglasses.

Breaking point
Polarizing filters similar to sunglasses are used to check weak points in plastic objects. When a plastic object is seen through the filters, colored bands appear in the places where it might break.

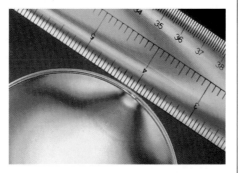

GROWTH

Living things are usually small when they start life. They grow and become adult. People and animals need food to make them grow. Plants grow too, and they also need food. Most plants make their own food from air, water, and sunlight. They use this food to grow stems and leaves, and sometimes to bear flowers and fruits. The leaves and fruits may then become food for people and animals.

Greatest growth
These trees are the biggest living things in the world. They are giant redwoods, which begin life as little seeds and can grow to 360 ft (110 m) tall.

Plant products
Many useful things are made from plants; clothes from cotton, for example, and paper from trees.

Bursting buds
Place some budding twigs in water. Soon, leaves and flowers will grow from the buds. These are horse chestnut twigs.

Good food
Growing plants provide food, such as these fruits and vegetables. Food products, such as bread and sugar, are made from plants.

Living parts
All living things are made of many tiny parts called cells. By looking at plants through a magnifying glass, you can see how they are formed. This is a magnified view of a moss plant.

Discover the needs of seeds

Seeds seem lifeless, but they can suddenly come alive and grow into plants. Show how they need three things for this; water, oxygen from the air, and warmth.

You will need:

Pitcher of water

Three deep saucers

Paper towels

Bowl of water

Mung bean seeds

1 Place the beans in the bowl of water and leave them to soak overnight.

2 Put paper towels in the saucers. You may need to fold them in two.

3 Pour a little water into the first saucer to moisten the towel.

4 Place some beans on the paper towel in each one of the three saucers.

5 Pour enough water into the second saucer to cover the beans.

Keep the beans covered by adding more water every day.

6 Leave the saucers in a warm place for several days. Only the beans in the first saucer begin to grow properly.

The dry beans get no water and do not begin to grow.

Keep the paper moist by adding a little water when necessary.

The underwater beans begin to grow, but the water stops air from getting to them and they stop growing.

These beans grow because they get water from the moist paper and oxygen from the air, and they are warm.

Growing crops

Farmers sow seeds of crop plants on the land. The seeds need water to start growing, and the young crops also need water to grow. If it does not rain, the seeds and plants must be given water. These crops are being sprayed with water. Watering crops is called "irrigation."

50 See how a plant grows

Most plants begin life beneath the ground. They grow from seeds, which drop into the soil. There is a way you can see what happens out of sight under the ground. A bean is the seed of a bean plant. You can grow it in a glass jar, where you can see it clearly.

You will need:

Pitcher of water

A dried bean

Blotting paper or paper towel

A tall glass jar

1 Roll up the blotting paper and place it in the jar. Put the bean between the paper and the jar. Wet the blotting paper. Keep the jar in a warm place.

2 After a few days, a root appears and grows downward. It is searching for water, which the bean needs to grow.

3 A green shoot comes out of the bean and grows upward. The shoot is looking for light, so it can grow. More roots grow down.

It helps to soak the bean in water for a day first.

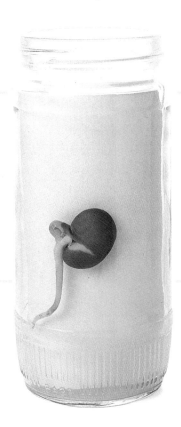

The paper should be kept moist, so add water when necessary.

At first, the bean uses its own store of food. Later, it uses light to make food.

Roots always grow down

Soak a bean in water for a day, then push a wire into it. (Ask an adult to help with this.) Fix the wire to the lid of the jar. Put some wet cotton balls in the jar, put in the bean, and close the jar. Lay the jar on its side and leave it for a few days until a root begins to grow down. Then turn the jar so the root points upward. Leave it, and the root changes direction so it grows down again.

The shoot is growing down after the bean has been turned.

51 Make a plant maze

Make a plant find its way through a maze! This shows how plants must have light in order to grow. They use the light to make food for themselves.

You will need:

Two pieces of card

Pitcher of water

Scissors

Runner bean seed

Pot of soil mix

Long cardboard box

1  Cut a large window in one end of the box.

2 Cut a window in each card.

3 Plant the bean seed in the pot and water it.

Soak the bean seed for a day before planting it.

4 Fit a piece of card in the box. Put the pot in the bottom.

5 Put the lid on and stand the box in a warm, light place.

The young plant always grows toward a source of light.

Tall trees
Getting enough light can be a problem for the plants in a thick forest. Many of the trees grow very tall, competing with each other for light. Their leaves make the forest beneath them quite dark, but some smaller types of trees and shrubs have adapted to this.

6 Insert the second piece of card when the plant grows.

7 The plant bends in order to get through all the windows and reach the light.

52 Grow a piece of plant

Plants do not grow only from seeds. You can cut up some plants, and new plants grow from the pieces! These are called "cuttings." Each one grows its own roots.

You will need:

Rubber band

Clear plastic bag

Pruners

Pot of moist soil mix

Geranium plant

1 Ask an adult to cut a side shoot from the plant. It should have leaves, but no flowers.

2 Plant this cutting in the pot. Cover it with the plastic bag.

Secure the bag with the rubber band.

3 Over several weeks, your cutting will grow into a new geranium plant. You must keep the compost moist.

53 See a plant bubble

Plants need light to make their own food. You can show that plants also produce oxygen, which enters the air and water. Oxygen is important because nothing can live without it.

You will need:

Wide jar

Pond weed

Funnel

Test tube

1 Submerge the jar, pond weed, funnel, and tube in a deep bowl of water. Then, still underwater, arrange them as the picture shows. When you remove them from the water, the test tube remains full.

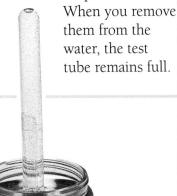

Oxygen from the weed rises to the top of the tube, pushing the water out.

2 Place the jar in sunlight. The pond weed begins to bubble!

Oxygen for life
It is important to have green water plants in an aquarium to release oxygen into the water. The fish breathe this oxygen. Green plants on dry land release oxygen into the air. The process in which plants use light to make food and oxygen is called "photosynthesis."

54 Test a plant for food

Plants make their own food in their leaves. This food is called "starch," and plants need it to grow. Test the leaves of a geranium plant to detect its food.

You will need:

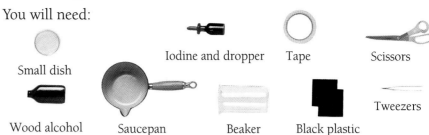

Small dish

Wood alcohol

Iodine and dropper

Tape

Scissors

Saucepan

Beaker

Black plastic

Tweezers

1 Tape plastic around some leaves. Place the geranium in a light place for two days. Then pick a wrapped leaf and an unwrapped leaf.

No light can get through the plastic. The leaf uses up all its starch and makes no more.

2 👥 Heat the water. Warm the wood alcohol in the beaker. Dip both the leaves in hot water, then leave them in the wood alcohol.

Putting the leaves in hot water and spirit removes the chlorophyll and makes them turn white.

3 Now the leaves are almost white. Add iodine to them. The unwrapped leaf goes dark. The wrapped one does not.

The substance that makes leaves green is called "chlorophyll." It helps the leaf make starch.

This green leaf has had no treatment. It still contains chlorophyll.

This is the wrapped leaf. It has no starch and so does not darken in iodine.

This is the unwrapped leaf. Treating it with iodine turns the starch in it a dark, blue-black color.

55 Grow your own mold

A fungus is a type of plant that does not produce seeds. Instead, it reproduces by releasing thousands of tiny specks called "spores" into the air. When the spores land, they grow into new fungi. Mold is an example of a fungus. You can grow some mold at home on bits of unwanted food.

You will need:

Two slices of bread

Peach

Yogurt

Five foil containers

Knife Spoon Chopping board Beans Clear food wrap

You can use other fruit instead, but mold grows quicker on moist fruit such as oranges and peaches than it does on drier fruit such as bananas.

1 👫 Carefully cut the peach in half on a chopping board. Then place the two halves in a foil container.

Make sure the toasted bread is very dry.

2 👫 Toast one slice of bread. Moisten the other slice with water. Cut the slices in half. Place the dry bread in the second foil container and the moist bread in the third.

3 Spoon some beans into the fourth container, and some yogurt into the fifth.

Keep the wet and dry bread separate.

Make sure that the containers are tightly wrapped.

4 Cover each container in clear food wrap. Leave the containers in a warm place for several days. Check on the containers every day, to see if anything has happened to the food.

Make spore prints

Mushrooms are fungi. New mushrooms grow from the spores shed by fully grown mushrooms. You can make some spore prints to see how the spores drop from the mushrooms. Take two flat mushrooms with dark undersides. Remove the stalks and place the mushrooms on a sheet of white paper, with their undersides facing downward. Leave them for a day or two. When you lift the mushrooms, you will notice that they leave patterns of dark powder on the paper.

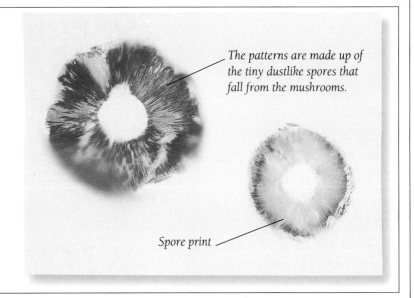

The patterns are made up of the tiny dustlike spores that fall from the mushrooms.

Spore print

5 Although you could not see them, tiny mold spores in the air landed on the different foods before you covered them up. After several days, mold will begin to appear on the food as the tiny mold spores grow. The mold grows faster on some foods than others. You may find that you get different colored mold on different types foods.

Make sure that you throw the moldy food away. Do not touch it and wear kitchen gloves when you handle the containers.

Moisture and warmth help the spores to feed on the dampened bread, so the mold grows well.

Mold needs moisture to grow, so no mold appears on the dry, toasted bread.

SENSES

Your senses are your ability to see, hear, smell and taste things, and to feel things when you touch them. Your senses make it possible for you to find out about the world around you, to do the things you want to do, and to survive. For example, your sight helps you see what is happening and find your way around.

Talking hands
One way to "talk" to someone who cannot hear is to use sign language. Deaf people watch the signs and use their sense of sight to understand what is being "said."

Bombarding the senses
Our senses bring us exciting experiences – such as the bright lights and music at a concert.

On the ball
Games bring the senses of sight, hearing, and touch into action. Good players use all these senses well, reacting quickly to the sight and sound of the ball or to the other players, and throwing the ball accurately.

A tasty sight
We use our senses of sight and touch to help us choose good food, such as these vegetables. We then use our senses of taste and smell to enjoy eating them.

56 See how your ears work

When a sound enters your ears, it is changed into a signal. This travels to your brain, and you hear the sound. You can build a model ear to see how your ears do this.

You will need:

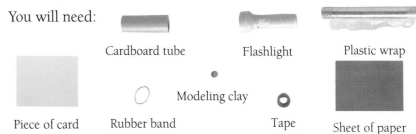

Cardboard tube   Flashlight   Plastic wrap

Modeling clay

Piece of card   Rubber band   Tape   Sheet of paper

1 Stretch the plastic wrap over the end of the tube. Secure it with the rubber band.

The film must be smooth.

2 Roll the sheet of paper to make a cone. Tape it together so that it does not unroll.

3 Push the small end of the cone into the open end of the cardboard tube. Tape it in place.

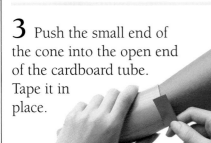

Fix the card with modeling clay.

4 Stand the card on a table top. Lay the tube in front of it. Shine the flashlight on the plastic wrap so that a spot of light appears on the card.

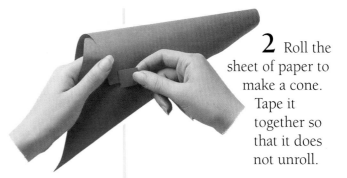

Inside the ear
As sounds enter the ear, the eardrum vibrates. This in turn makes tiny bones vibrate and the vibration passes to the inner ear, which then sends signals to the brain, along the ear's nerve.

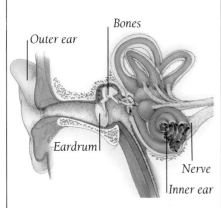

Outer ear   Bones

Eardrum

Nerve

Inner ear

The light is reflected from the wrap. As it vibrates, the spot of light shakes.

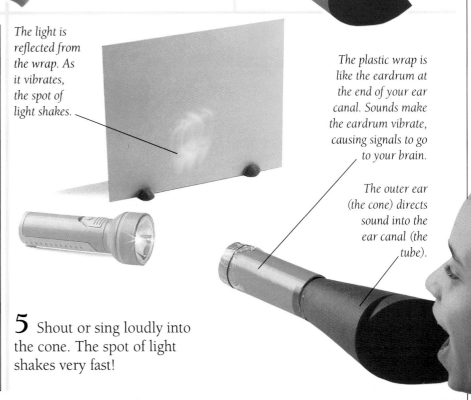

The plastic wrap is like the eardrum at the end of your ear canal. Sounds make the eardrum vibrate, causing signals to go to your brain.

The outer ear (the cone) directs sound into the ear canal (the tube).

5 Shout or sing loudly into the cone. The spot of light shakes very fast!

57 Find out how your eyes work

Build a model eye using a magnifying glass and a goldfish bowl, and find out how you see. Use the model to show how the eye forms an image of a human figure.

You will need:

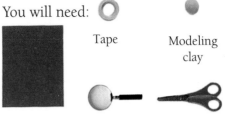

Tape

Modeling clay

Tissue paper

Card   Magnifying glass   Scissors   Flashlight   Goldfish bowl of water

1 Tape the tissue to the side of the bowl.

2 Hold the magnifying glass in front of the bowl using the clay.

3 Fold the card and cut out half of a figure.

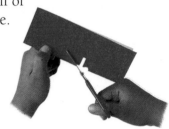

4 Attach the card in front of the magnifying glass.

You have a lens like a magnifying glass in each eye.

The flashlight lights up the figure in front of the model eye.

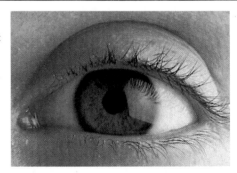

The round bowl is like your eyeball.

The tissue is like the retina at the back of each eye.

The lens bends the light rays from the figure to form an image.

5 Shine the flashlight on the figure. An upside-down image of it appears on the tissue. Move the magnifying glass back and forth to make the image sharp.

The image forms on the retina, which sends signals to the brain so that you see the figure.

Entry to the eye
At the center of each eye, there is a hole called the "pupil," where light enters the eye. The pupil changes size to control the amount of light entering the eye. If there is not much light, it gets larger and lets more in.

58 See two pictures as one

Trick your eyes into seeing one picture when there are really two – one on each side of a piece of card. This experiment shows how you can see moving pictures on television and in the movies.

You will need:

Scissors   Compass   Colored markers   Two rubber bands   White card

1 Make a circle on the card, using the compass. Cut it out.

2 Draw a circle on the card. Make two holes, one on each side.

3 Turn the card over and draw a cross on the other side.

4 Thread a rubber band through each of the holes in the card.

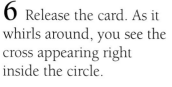

5 Twist the bands by holding them and turning the card.

6 Release the card. As it whirls around, you see the cross appearing right inside the circle.

The card whirls so fast that images of the circle and cross overlap in your eyes.

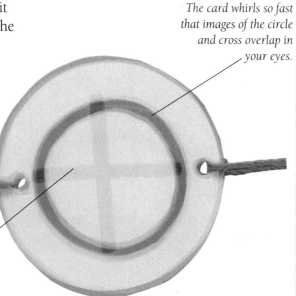

Your eyes hold an image of an object for a short time after the object disappears.

Moving pictures

Movies are made up of long strips of still pictures, each one slightly different from the one before. The pictures appear rapidly on the screen, one after the other. When you watch a movie, your eyes do not see each picture separately. They overlap and appear to move.

59 Build a wobble detector

Having two eyes helps you judge distances well. With a wobble detector, you can find out just how useful it is to have two eyes. Close one eye and you'll find you can't help wobbling!

You will need:

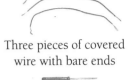

Two jar lids   Bare stiff wire   Scissors   Three pieces of covered wire with bare ends

Bulb-holder and bulb   Modeling clay   Tape   Battery   Screwdriver

1 Use modeling clay to attach the ends of the stiff wire to the jar lids.

Bend the stiff wire into several curves.

2 Using one piece of covered wire, connect one end of the stiff wire to the battery.

3 Connect the second piece of covered wire to the battery and the bulb-holder.

4 Take the last piece of covered wire and attach one end to the bulb-holder. Make a loop with the other end.

5 Place the loop around the stiff wire. Try to move the loop along the wire without touching it. Try it with both eyes open, then with one eye closed. Which is easier?

The loop is made with bare wire.

With only one eye, you cannot judge the position of the loop. It is much harder not to wobble.

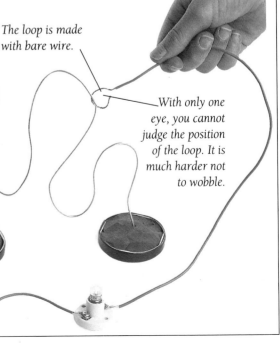

Looking forward to a meal
An owl has two large eyes that face forward. These help the owl judge the position of the prey it is hunting. Like the owl, you use two eyes to see how near or how far objects are. Your brain combines the images from both eyes to do this.

60 Change your ears around

Sounds come to you from all sides. Having two ears makes it possible to figure out where sounds are coming from. Trick your hearing so sounds come from the wrong directions.

You will need:

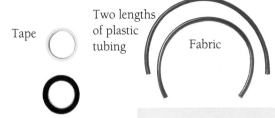

Tape

Two lengths of plastic tubing

Fabric

Two plastic funnels

Insulating tape

Length of wood

1 Fix each tube to a funnel. Tape the tubes to the wood, as the picture shows. Fit the tubes into your ears so they fit closely. Do not force them in.

Attach fabric over the end of each tube.

2 Ask a friend to walk by, making a noise. The sounds seem to move the opposite way to your friend!

A sound from one side goes to the ear on the other side.

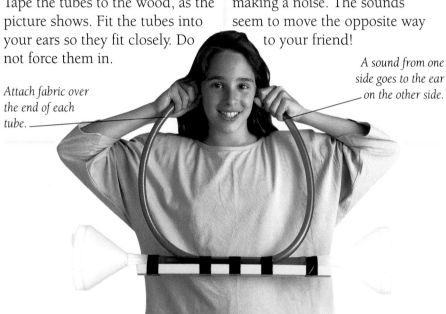

Steering by sound

A bat uses its sense of hearing to find its way around in the dark. As it flies, it makes high sounds that are almost impossible for our ears to hear. These sounds bounce off nearby objects and return to the bat's ears. The bat uses these returning sounds to locate objects around it – and to find the insects it hunts for food.

61 Take a taste test

If you test your sense of taste, you will find that it is not just your mouth that enables you to tell one flavor from another – your sense of smell is very important, too.

You will need:

Three small glasses

Three different types of pure fruit juice

Large glass of water

Scarf

1 Ask a friend to blindfold you with the scarf. Taste each juice in turn. You will find it easy to recognize the flavors.

Wash your mouth out between tastings.

2 Hold your nose and taste the juices again. Now it is more difficult to identify the juices!

The juices now have similar flavors.

62 Test your sense of touch

You can feel something as soon as it touches your skin, but you may not be able to detect its shape or size. Make a touch tester to find out just how much you can feel.

You will need:

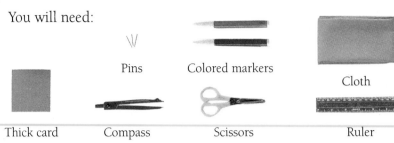

Pins   Colored markers

Cloth

Thick card   Compass   Scissors   Ruler

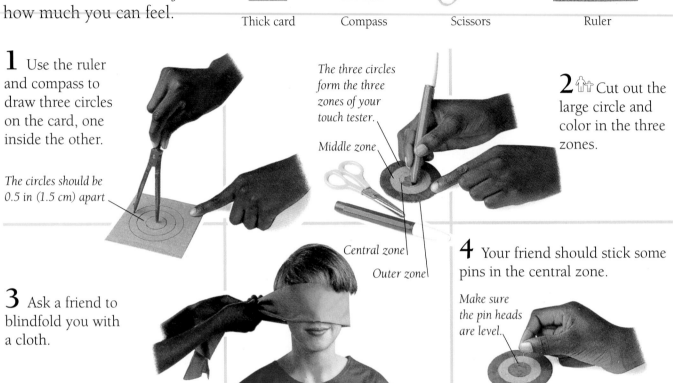

1 Use the ruler and compass to draw three circles on the card, one inside the other.

The circles should be 0.5 in (1.5 cm) apart

The three circles form the three zones of your touch tester.

Middle zone

Central zone

Outer zone

2 Cut out the large circle and color in the three zones.

3 Ask a friend to blindfold you with a cloth.

4 Your friend should stick some pins in the central zone.

Make sure the pin heads are level.

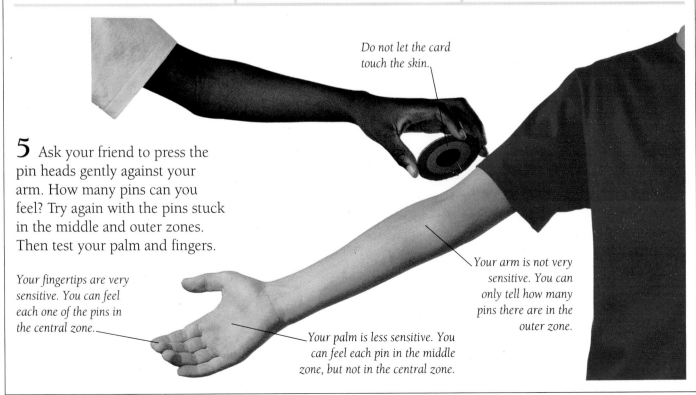

Do not let the card touch the skin.

5 Ask your friend to press the pin heads gently against your arm. How many pins can you feel? Try again with the pins stuck in the middle and outer zones. Then test your palm and fingers.

Your fingertips are very sensitive. You can feel each one of the pins in the central zone.

Your palm is less sensitive. You can feel each pin in the middle zone, but not in the central zone.

Your arm is not very sensitive. You can only tell how many pins there are in the outer zone.

63 Check your reaction time

You need all your senses to tell you when you suddenly have to take action. Sometimes you need to move very fast. Do this test to find out just how quick off the mark you really are.

You will need:

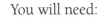
Pencil

Colored markers

White paper

Scissors

Glue

12 in (30 cm) ruler

1 Draw around the ruler on the paper. Cut out the strip and mark six equal bands.

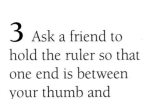

2 Color the bands and then glue the strip to the ruler.

3 Ask a friend to hold the ruler so that one end is between your thumb and your forefinger.

Keep your thumb and forefinger about 0.5 in (1.5 cm) apart.

Slow reaction time

4 Suddenly, your friend releases the ruler. Try to catch it! The color you grab tells you your reaction time.

Medium reaction time

Fast reaction time

Your reaction time is the time between sensing something and beginning to move.

Wait for it!
As soon as the kitten sees the yarn move, it darts into action and begins to chase it, just like an adult cat after its prey. Animals often have very fast reactions. They need these when they are hunting for food, or escaping from enemies.

SOUND AND MUSIC

Sounds are all around us. There are beautiful sounds in nature – such as birds singing and water lapping. There are frightening sounds too, like thunder. We use sounds when we speak to each other, and music brings us great pleasure. A siren makes a sound that warns us of danger. There are so many different sounds – but none of them is anything more than a shaking movement in the air.

Sound signals
We often use sounds as signals. Blowing a whistle in a game can mean "stop" or "go."

Sound pictures
This is a picture of an unborn baby – inside its mother! The picture was made using special sounds called "ultrasound."

The speed of sound
You hear the bang a balloon makes as soon as it bursts. This is because sound travels quickly from the balloon to your ears. It moves at 1,115 ft (340 m) per second – slightly faster than most airliners.

Songs of the sea
Many animals make sounds to communicate with one another. Whales' "songs" can travel quite far underwater.

Making music
Music is fun, whether you listen to it, play it, or sing. You can make good music with homemade instruments such as this drum. Experiment 69 (page 80) explains how to make it.

64 See some sound

When anything makes a sound, it "vibrates" or shakes rapidly. This makes the air around it vibrate, too. Air vibrations, called "sound waves," spread out through the air. When they reach your ears, you hear a sound. Show how sounds make the air shake.

You will need:

Rubber band   Plastic bowl   Big saucepan   Piece of heavy plastic

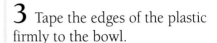

Uncooked rice   Scissors   Large spoon   Tape

1 👫 Cut a piece of plastic slightly bigger than the bowl.

2 Stretch the plastic over the bowl, using the rubber band to hold it in place.

3 Tape the edges of the plastic firmly to the bowl.

Stretch the plastic as tightly as you can.

5 Hold the saucepan near the plastic. Hit it with a spoon. The rice jumps up and down!

As you hit it, the pan vibrates and gives out sound waves.

4 Sprinkle a few grains of the rice on the stretched plastic.

Sound waves travel through the air and make the plastic vibrate.

Getting the vibrations

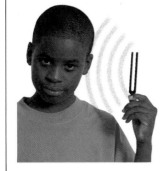

This picture shows a boy listening to a tuning fork. The tuning fork is giving out sound waves. If you could see the air vibrations in sound waves, they would look like the blue curves. Thousands of these vibrations reach your ears every second as you hear a sound.

The grains of rice jump up and down as the plastic vibrates. You can see this clearly from the side.

65 Make a sound gun

Sound waves batter your ears – though you may not feel them. Loud sounds can make things move. Prove this by firing a sound wave at a target and making it shake.

You will need:

Scissors

Thin plastic Cardboard tube   Stiff paper

Thin strip of paper   Rubber band

Sharp pencil   Tape

1 Draw around the tube to make a circle on the paper.

2 👭 Cut out the circle from the paper.

3 👭 Use the sharp end of the pencil to make a small hole in the center of the circle.

4 Tape the circle to one end of the tube.

5 Using the rubber band, fix the plastic over the other end.

6 Fold the paper strip and tape it to a table top.

Sliding snow
Sound can cause an "avalanche" – when ice and snow crash down the side of a mountain. Sound waves from a loud noise disturb the snow and start it moving.

7 Point the end of the tube with the hole at the paper strip. Tap the plastic and the strip shakes.

Tapping the plastic causes a sound wave to travel down the tube.

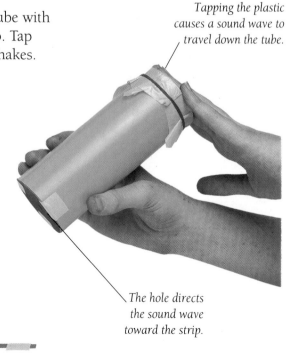

The sound wave makes the air move and shake the strip.

The hole directs the sound wave toward the strip.

66 Make a coat-hanger clanger

Sound waves travel through other materials as well as through air – and sometimes much better. This simple experiment uses cotton thread to carry sounds to your ears.

You will need:

Scissors

Ruler

Cotton thread

Coat hanger

1 Measure out and cut two pieces of thread 12 in (30 cm) long. Tie one end of each thread to the base of the coat hanger.

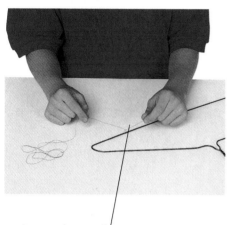

When you have tied the threads, slide them to opposite corners of the hanger.

As the coat hanger bangs against the chair, it makes a gentle ringing sound.

2 Wind one thread around the index finger of each hand. Lift the hanger up by the threads and then swing it against a chair. Listen to the noise it makes.

Sound travels more efficiently up the thread to your ears than it does through the air.

Sounds in your head
Strike a tuning fork on a table. Gently press the base against your head. The sound is louder than when you first heard it! Like the thread in the above experiment, the bones of your skull carry sounds to your ears much better than the air.

3 Put the fingers wrapped in cotton in your ears, but do not press them in too hard. Swing the hanger against the chair again. Now the hanger sounds like the clanging of a huge bell!

67 Bounce a sound

Sometimes, you hear sounds that have not come straight to you. Show how sounds may reach your ears after they have first bounced off another object.

You will need:

Ticking watch

Two cardboard tubes

Plate

Cork mat

Several books

1 Build two piles of books, both the same height.

2 Lay one tube on each of the piles of books.

3 Hold the watch close to one ear and check that it ticks.

4 Place the watch in the end of one of the tubes.

5 Listen at the end of the other tube. You cannot hear the watch tick – until a friend holds the plate near the ends of the tubes.

Sound waves travel down the tube to the plate.

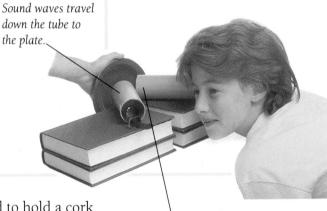

The sound waves bounce off the hard plate and travel up the tube to your ears.

Good sounds

In a concert hall, sound waves from the stage bounce off the walls. This helps improve the quality of the sound the audience hears.

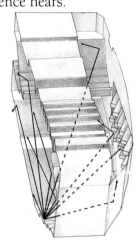

6 Get your friend to hold a cork mat instead of the plate. Now you cannot hear the watch any more.

The soft cork soaks up the sound waves.

68 Make a paper banger

Make a loud bang with nothing more than a sheet of paper! The banger produces a quick and large movement of air, forming a sudden and powerful sound wave. This rushes through the air toward you and you hear it as a bang.

You will need:

A sheet of stiff paper measuring about 16 in by 12 in (30 cm by 40 cm)

1 Fold the longer edges of the paper together. Then open it out.

Fold here

2 Fold the corners into the first fold.

First fold

3 Fold the paper in half along the first fold. Then fold it in half again, lengthways.

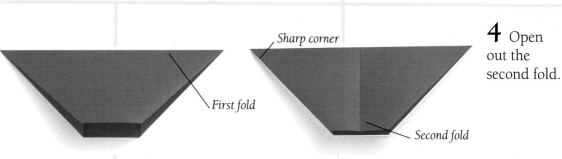

First fold

Sharp corner

4 Open out the second fold.

Second fold

Thunder and lightning
A flash of lightning heats the air so that it expands very suddenly. This sends a powerful sound wave through the air. We hear this as a clap of thunder.

5 Fold down the two sharp corners.

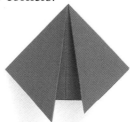

6 Fold the paper back along the second fold to make a triangle shape.

7 Grip the banger firmly by the two sharp corners. Flick it down quickly – and it makes a loud bang!

A flap of paper springs out and makes the air move suddenly. You hear this as a bang.

69 Beat some drums

Make a tin drum and a tom-tom. They make different kinds of sounds, but they work in the same way. When you hit a drum's stretched skin, it vibrates. This makes the air inside the drum vibrate – and out comes the sound.

You will need:

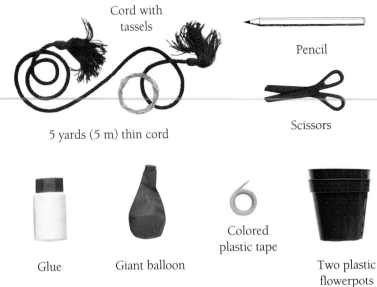

Cord with tassels

Pencil

5 yards (5 m) thin cord

Scissors

Glue   Giant balloon   Colored plastic tape   Two plastic flowerpots

Colored paper

White cotton muslin

Round cookie tin

1 Decorate the tin with colored paper. Tape the thick cord firmly to opposite sides of the tin.

2 Cut off the balloon's neck. Stretch the balloon over the tin and tape it. The tin drum is ready.

3 Using the pot, draw two circles on the muslin. Then draw two larger circles around each one.

4 Cover the pots with coloured paper. Then tape the bottoms of the pots firmly together.

5 Cut out the large circles of muslin. Cut slits in each edge, as far as the second circle.

6 Fold in and glue the flaps of both circles. With the pencil, make 16 holes around each edge.

Make sure the holes are evenly spaced.

7 Thread thin cord through the holes. Place a circle over each pot. Pull the cord tight and tie it.

8 Zigzag the rest of the cord through the cords at the edges of the circles. Pull it tight and tie it.

9 Spread glue over each circle. Tighten the cord again. When the glue is dry, the tom-tom is ready.

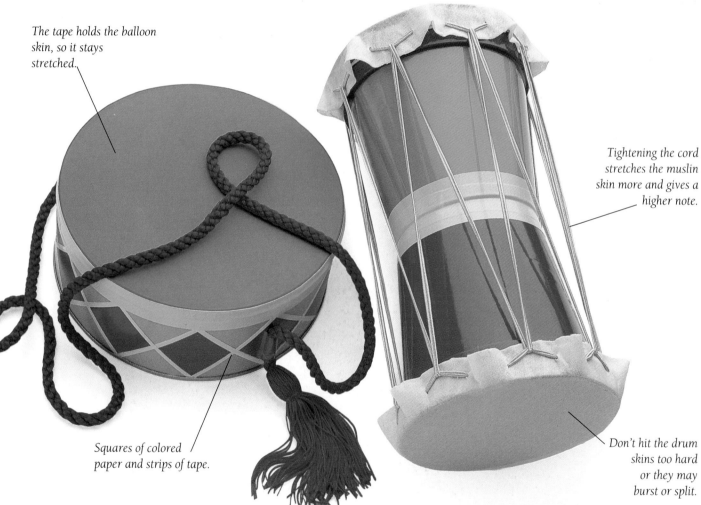

The tape holds the balloon skin, so it stays stretched.

Tightening the cord stretches the muslin skin more and gives a higher note.

Squares of colored paper and strips of tape.

Don't hit the drum skins too hard or they may burst or split.

Drum set
This is the standard drum set played by a drummer in a band. It has several drums of different sizes, and the drummer plays them all – including a large drum played with a foot pedal. It also has several cymbals.

10 Put the cord of the tin drum around your neck. Beat the drum with a stick, such as a pencil. Hold the tom-tom under your arm or between your knees. Beat it with your fingers.

70 Strike up a tune

Make your own xylophone. This instrument has wooden bars that vibrate, producing musical notes when you strike them. Your xylophone is made with pencils.

You will need:

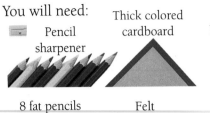

Pencil sharpener

8 fat pencils

Thick colored cardboard

Felt

Poster paint

Glue

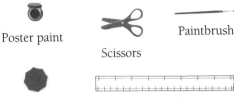

Scissors

Paintbrush

Ruler

1 Use the shapes below to make a cardboard frame. Paint it and glue felt along the ridges.

Make the sides of the frame this shape 8.5 in (21 cm) long.

Make the long end of the frame this shape 6 in (15 cm) long.

2 Use the sharpener to shorten the pencils as shown. Rest them on the frame.

These shapes are smaller than the ones you need. Make yours the sizes shown.

3 Play the pencil xylophone with beaters made from wooden skewers and beads.

Make the short end of the frame this shape 4.5 in (11 cm) long.

71 Play a pipe

You can make music from a set of pipes. All you have to do is blow across the open ends. This makes the air inside each pipe vibrate, producing a musical note. Different lengths of pipes give different notes.

You will need:

Card

Glue

Scissors

Colored tapes

5 ft (1.5 m) plastic pipe

Colored ribbon

Modeling clay

1 Cut the pipe into pieces, each 0.5 in (1 cm) longer than the last. Decorate them with tape.

2 Tape the pipes together to make a set. Glue the ribbon to a strip of card, and glue it over the tape.

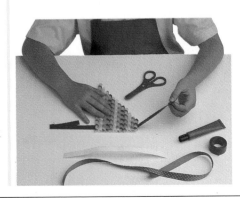

3 Roll the clay into small balls. Push one ball of clay into the bottom of each pipe.

Shorter pipes give higher notes.

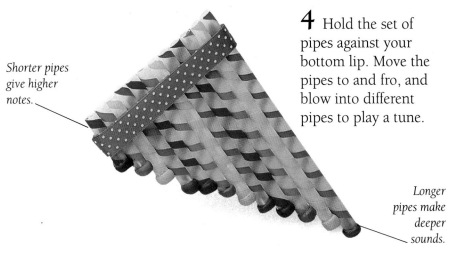

4 Hold the set of pipes against your bottom lip. Move the pipes to and fro, and blow into different pipes to play a tune.

Longer pipes make deeper sounds.

72 Blow a horn

You can make a horn from a hose and a funnel! Close your lips firmly together and put them to the end of the horn. Blow air through your lips and the horn will sound. This happens because your lips make the air inside the horn vibrate.

You will need:

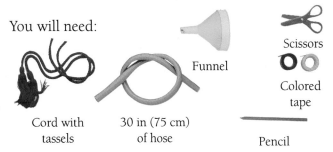

Scissors

Funnel

Colored tape

Cord with tassels

30 in (75 cm) of hose

Pencil

1 Decorate the funnel with tape. Push it into one end of the hose and secure it with tape.

2 Tape around the other end to make the mouthpiece. Loop the hose and attach the pencil to it.

3 Decorate the horn with strips of tape and the cord. Now your horn is ready to blow.

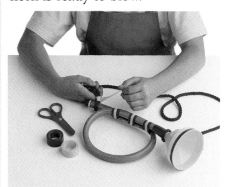

Blow through the mouthpiece.

The horn produces only a few notes. You can get these by pressing your lips tighter together as you blow, or letting them relax a little.

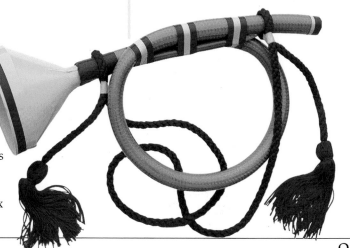

73 Build a banjo

A banjo has four strings, stretched tightly. You play the banjo by plucking the strings with your fingers. The strings vibrate very fast, producing musical notes. You can strum a rhythm by plucking all the strings together. Or you can play one note after another, to pick out a tune. You can make each string play several notes.

You will need:

Pen
Scissors
Poster paints
Big balloon
10 ft (3 m) fishing line
Colored ribbons
Length of wood
Colored plastic tape
Colored paper
Round, plastic ice-cream tub
Four thumbtacks
Eight eyelet screws
Paintbrush
Glue
Stiff card
Clear glaze

1 Cut two 'I' shapes under the rim of the tub, opposite each other. Make them as wide as the end of the wood.

2 Bend the flaps of the 'I' shapes out. Push the end of the wood through the holes. Tack the flaps to the wood.

3 Paint and glaze the wood and the tub. Mix glue with the paint you use for the tub. Paint lines across the wood.

4 Cut off the neck of the balloon. Stretch the balloon over the tub and tape it to the sides. Paint a design on it.

5 Partly screw four eyelet screws into each end of the wood. Make sure you can turn each screw in either direction.

6 Make two triangular bridges of card and paper. Make one the same width as the wood and the other three times as wide.

7  Make four strings by cutting the fishing line. Tie these strings securely to the two sets of eyelet screws.

8 Insert the two bridges under the strings, as the picture shows. Turn the eyelet screws to tighten the strings.

Hold a string down to change its note. The notes get higher as you move your hand toward the tub. The lines show you where to press the strings.

9 Decorate the banjo by tying pieces of ribbon of different colors to the eyelet screws. Your banjo is now ready to play.

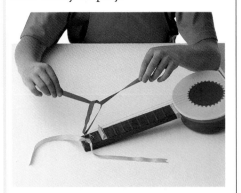

Tightening the string makes it sound higher. Slightly loosening the string lowers its note.

Make each bridge by folding and gluing pieces of card and paper. Cut four notches in one edge to hold the strings.

The bridges raise the strings so they are free to vibrate.

10 Tune the banjo by tightening the strings, so each one gives a different note.

Busy fingers
The guitar is like a banjo, except that it has six strings. When you press a guitar or banjo string, you change the length of the part of the string that vibrates. This changes the note made by the string when you pluck it.

MAGNETS

Magnets have mysterious powers. They can pull things toward them and push other magnets away. This power drives the electric motors that are inside many machines we use – such as hairdryers and trains. Magnets make it possible for television sets, radios, and tape players to produce sounds. Computers use magnets to store information.

Lights in the sky
The Earth is a huge magnet. Its magnetism makes these colored lights appear in the sky near the north and south poles.

Magnetic mineral
The first magnets were pieces of black mineral called "lodestone." Lodestone attracts objects such as this paper clip.

North, south, east, west
You use a compass to find directions. It makes use of the Earth's magnetism, which causes the needle always to point north.

Pick and stick
A magnet can pick up objects made of iron or steel. The objects stick to the ends of the magnets.

Music with magnets
The tapes you listen to are made using magnets. The tape player and the earphones that go with it contain magnets.

Flying home
Pigeons can usually find their way home. Some scientists believe they use the Earth's magnetism to sense direction, much like a compass.

74 Charm a snake, fly a kite

Make a snake rear up and raise a kite into the sky – all with the amazing power of magnets. At the same time, you can find out which kinds of things magnets attract.

You will need:

Tape

Selection of magnets

Scissors

Small objects, paper clips, and a pencil

Sewing thread

Glue

Ruler

Colored felt

Snake pattern

1 👭 Copy the snake pattern onto felt. Cut out the snake and decorate it with colored felt.

2 Tie a short length of thread to a paper clip. Fix the paper clip to the snake's head.

The magnet attracts the paper clip. Raise the magnet so that the paper clip pulls the thread tight.

3 Tape a magnet to the end of the ruler. Tape the loose end of the thread firmly to the table.

5 Hold a magnet close to the objects. See how it picks up only the ones made of iron and steel.

4 Move the ruler and magnet around, above the snake. The snake rises and dances, like a snake-charmer's snake. If the snake does not rise, use a stronger magnet or a shorter thread. Try making other shapes in the same way – like this brightly colored felt kite.

75 Compare the strength of magnets

Some magnets are stronger than others. This experiment shows you how to test a magnet's strength and compare the strengths of different combinations of magnets.

You will need:

 Rubber band

Small plastic lid

Two bar magnets

Washable-ink pen

Paper clip

Wooden skewers

Meat baster

Glass beaker

Cup of water

1 Place an upright bar magnet between two wooden skewers, midway along their lengths. Loop rubber bands over the skewers to hold the magnet tightly in place.

2 Add water to the glass beaker until it is about one-third full. Put the paper clip in the plastic lid. Gently place the lid on the water's surface so that it floats.

3 Rest the wooden skewers holding the magnet on the rim of the beaker. Make sure that the bottom end of the magnet is positioned over the plastic lid.

4 Using the baster, carefully add drops of water to the beaker. Stop adding water when the paper clip jumps up and clings to the magnet.

5 Mark the water level on the outside of the beaker. Repeat the experiment using two magnets. Make sure the magnets' repelling ends are alongside each other.

6 This time, the water level is much lower. Two magnets are stronger than one, so less water has to be added before they pull the paper clip toward them.

Underwater magnets

This diver is under the sea, checking part of an oil rig for damage. The cables used in these tests are held in place by the red magnets. These magnets are strong enough to stick to the steel rig, even though it is deep underwater.

76 Build a magnetic car

You can use two ordinary magnets to make a toy car move. It works because two magnets can either attract or repel each other when they are brought close together. The way in which they move depends on which ends of the magnets are facing each other.

You will need:

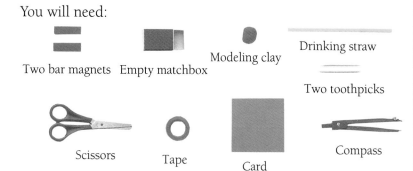

Two bar magnets Empty matchbox Modeling clay Drinking straw

Scissors Tape Card Two toothpicks Compass

1 Firmly tape one of the magnets to the inside of the tray of the matchbox.

2 Cut the straw in two pieces. Make each piece the same size as the matchbox.

3 Tape the pieces of straw to the outside part of the matchbox. Slide in the tray.

4 Using the compass, draw four identical circles on the card. Carefully cut them out.

5 Push the toothpicks through the straws. Attach the card circles to them.

Put clay over the sharp points.

The magnet in the car is attracted or repelled by the magnet in your hand.

Turn the magnet around, and the car rolls in the other direction.

6 Place the matchbox car on a tabletop. Bring the other magnet close. The car rolls toward or away from the magnet.

77 Detect a magnet's field

Around every magnet, there is a "magnetic field" where the magnet can exert its powers to push or pull. Normally, a magnetic field is invisible – but there is a way you can see it.

You will need:

Glass or plastic containers

Syrup

Pencil

String

Bar magnets and horseshoe magnets

Iron filings

Clear food wrap

1 Pour a dessert spoon of iron filings into a jar of syrup. Stir it well, mixing the filings evenly. Then pour some mixture into two clear glass or plastic containers.

2 Place two bar magnets under one container. Place two horseshoe magnets at opposite sides of the other.

3 Fill the third container with the mixture. Wrap a bar magnet in clear food wrap. Tie it with string to a pencil and then hang it in the container.

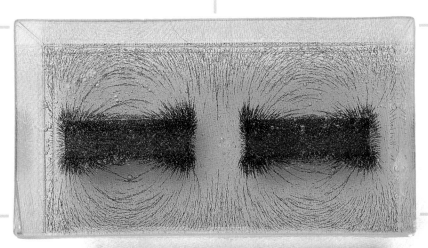

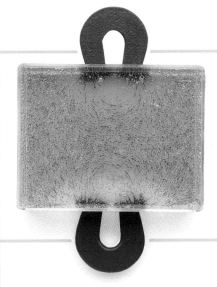

What do you see?
The filings form a pattern within the magnets' magnetic fields. The pattern shows you the direction of the pull from the magnets on the iron filings.

The two bar magnets are pushing each other away. The pattern of the filings shows how the two magnetic fields are working in opposite directions, keeping the magnets apart.

The two horseshoe magnets at opposite ends of a container both attract iron filings. The filings show how the magnetic fields loop around from one end of each magnet to the other end.

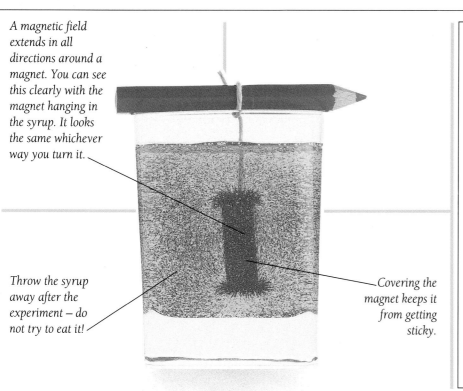

A magnetic field extends in all directions around a magnet. You can see this clearly with the magnet hanging in the syrup. It looks the same whichever way you turn it.

Throw the syrup away after the experiment – do not try to eat it!

Covering the magnet keeps it from getting sticky.

Magnetic attraction
A magnet can pick up a whole chain of small, steel objects. The magnet's field turns each one of the objects into a small magnet, which goes on to attract another steel object.

78 Separate a mixture

It is usually very difficult to separate two powders that have been mixed together. But you can do it easily if one of the powders is magnetic and the other is not.

You will need:

Plate of iron filings

Magnet

Plate of sand

1 Tip the plate of iron filings so that they drop into the sand. Stir them together with your fingers.

2 Keep stirring until the sand and the iron filings are completely mixed up.

3 Bring a magnet close to the plate. It will pick up the iron filings and leave the sand behind.

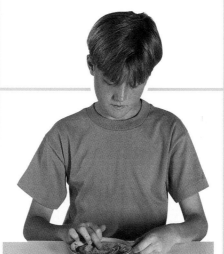

79 Construct a compass

The Earth is a huge magnet with its own magnetic field. This field is strong enough to make another magnet turn if it is free to move. A magnet will always turn to point north.

You will need:

Knife

Needle

Styrofoam pad

Pitcher of water

Bar magnet

Toothpick

Modeling clay

Compass

Tape

Plastic container

1 Use the compass to draw a circular disk on the styrofoam. Carefully cut it out and color it.

The disk must fit inside the container

2 Stick a blob of clay in the middle of the container. Push the toothpick upright in it.

3 Stroke one end of the magnet along the needle, about 30 times, in the same direction.

The needle becomes a magnet.

4 Tape the needle to the disk. Rest the disk on the stick. Fill the container with water.

North pole of the Earth's magnetic field

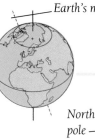

North pole

When the needle is magnetized, one end gains a north pole. The north pole of the Earth's magnetic field attracts the north pole of the needle.

South pole

Getting directions

The needle of a compass is a light magnet balancing on a pivot. As you turn the compass around, the needle will always swing to point north. If you turn the compass until "N" for north is below the needle, it will show all directions correctly.

5 When water reaches the disk, it floats and turns. One end of the needle points north, as a compass needle does. Mark this end.

80 Make an electromagnet

You can make a strong magnet by using electricity. It is not like an ordinary magnet, which is always magnetic. You can switch the power of an electromagnet on and off.

You will need:

Wire strippers

Scissors

Switch
(see experiment 87)

4.5V battery

Lots of paper clips

Plastic tape

Long screwdriver

6 ft (2 m) coated wire

1 👭 Cut a long piece of wire. Strip the ends and tape part of it to the handle of the screwdriver.

2 Coil most of the rest of the wire around the screwdriver. Tape the last turn.

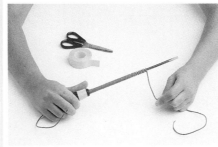

3 Connect the wire, and another short piece of wire, to the battery and switch, as the picture shows.

4 The screwdriver is now an electromagnet. Press the switch, and the screwdriver picks up some paper clips! Open the switch, and the paper clips fall off.

The paper clips contain steel wire that is attracted to the electromagnet.

Connect the short wire to the other terminal.

Electromagnet with 60 turns

Electromagnet with 40 turns

Electromagnet with 20 turns

The coil of wire produces a magnetic field when electricity flows through it. More turns of wire make a stronger field.

Metal mover

This crane has a powerful electromagnet to lift bits of scrap iron and steel. The scrap sticks to the electromagnet when it is switched on, and can be moved by the crane. When the current is switched off, the scrap falls away.

81 Build a buzzer

A buzzer uses magnetism to make a loud buzzing sound. It contains an electromagnet, like the one on page 93. The buzzer's button is a kind of switch. When you press it, electricity can travel to the electromagnet in the buzzer. The electromagnet causes movements within the buzzer. These movements make the noise.

You will need:

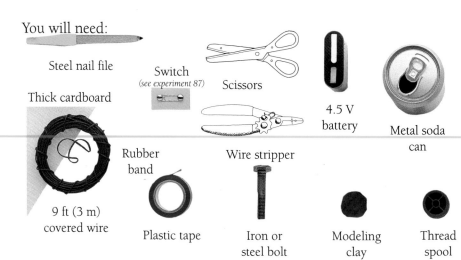

Steel nail file

Switch
(see experiment 87)

Scissors

Thick cardboard

Rubber band

Wire stripper

4.5 V battery

Metal soda can

9 ft (3 m) covered wire

Plastic tape

Iron or steel bolt

Modeling clay

Thread spool

1 Strip both ends of the wire. Wrap it firmly around the bolt 200 times. Fix the bolt to the cardboard with clay.

2 Using the rubber band, attach the handle of the nail file firmly to the spool.

4 Tape one end of the wire to the metal part of the nail file. Fix the spool to the cardboard, as shown in the next picture.

3 With the scissors, scrape away some paint at the base of the can. Do this again on the opposite side of the can.

You must remove the paint from the can, otherwise it would keep the electricity from getting to the electromagnet.

Hold the spool and flick the nail file. It should vibrate to and fro several times.

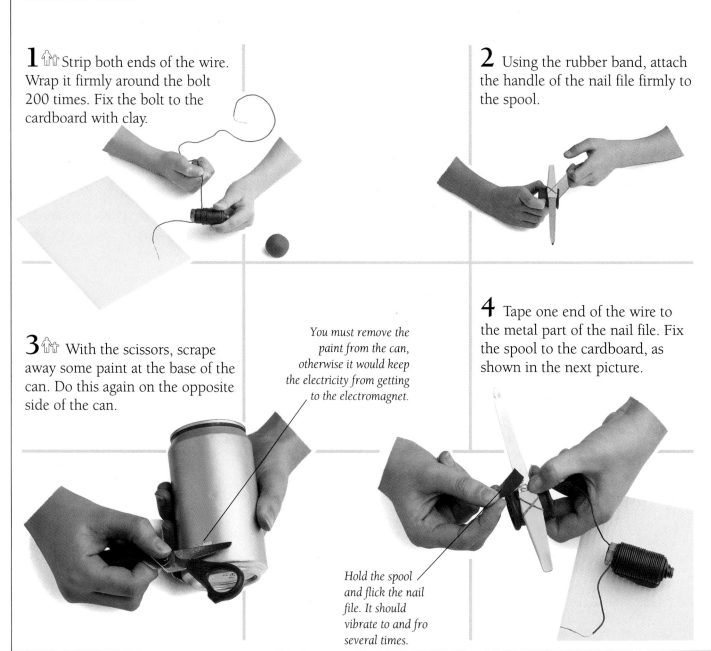

5 👥 Cut two wires and strip the ends. Attach one wire to the battery and the can and the other to the battery and the switch.

Tape the wire to the scraped part of the can.

6 Stick the can to the card, with the end of the nail file touching the other scraped part. Connect the switch, as the picture shows.

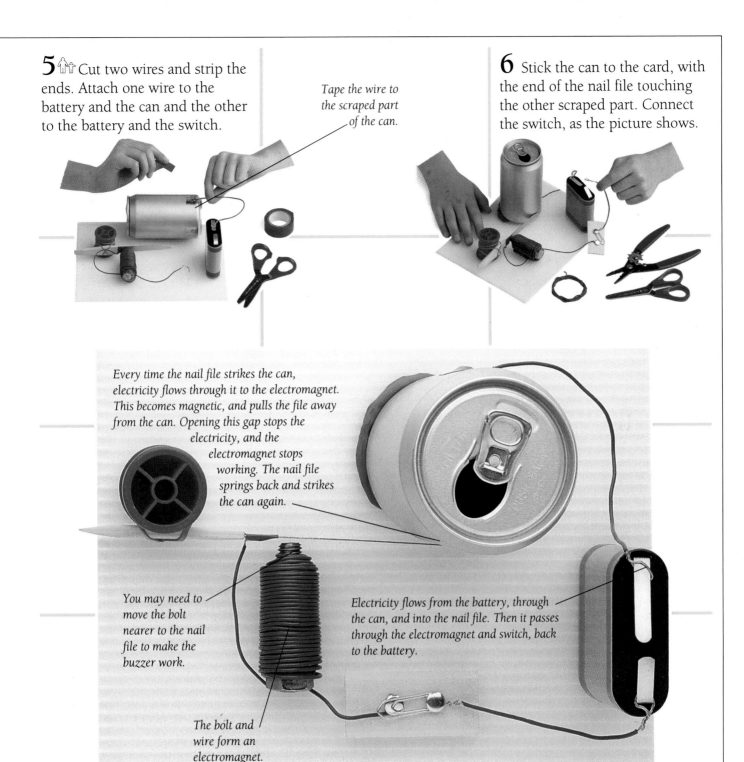

Every time the nail file strikes the can, electricity flows through it to the electromagnet. This becomes magnetic, and pulls the file away from the can. Opening this gap stops the electricity, and the electromagnet stops working. The nail file springs back and strikes the can again.

You may need to move the bolt nearer to the nail file to make the buzzer work.

Electricity flows from the battery, through the can, and into the nail file. Then it passes through the electromagnet and switch, back to the battery.

The bolt and wire form an electromagnet.

7 Press the switch, and a loud buzz comes from the can! The nail file vibrates rapidly to and fro and strikes the can again and again. When you release the switch, the nail file stops – and so does the buzzing.

Magnetic machine
Modern telephones work much like a buzzer does. Inside the earpiece there is a small electromagnet. When electricity flows through the electromagnet, it causes a strip of metal to vibrate. This vibration produces the sound of the caller's voice.

ELECTRICITY

Electricity makes all kinds of machines work. It can have great power – it drives the fastest trains in the world, for example. But electricity can also power very small machines, such as cassette players and calculators. Most machines you use at home, such as televisions and vacuum cleaners, use "current electricity." This is the kind of electricity that comes from batteries and power points in your home. There is another kind of electricity, called "static electricity," which you can make yourself.

Power from water
The electricity we use in our homes is made in power stations. This one is a "hydroelectric" power station. It uses the energy of moving water, coming through a dam.

Plug into power
You plug electrical machines like this hairdryer in to power points. Electricity travels from power stations along wires and into the power points.

Electric ride
These amusement park cars pick up current electricity from overhead wires. In each car, the electricity powers an electric motor that turns the wheels.

Electrical attraction
If you rub a balloon on a T-shirt or your hair, it gets static electricity on its surface. This causes it to stick to things: walls, ceilings, even you!

82 Bend some water

When you rub some objects, they gain electricity. This electricity stays in the objects, so it is called "static," which means it is something that stays in the same place. Static electricity has amazing power to attract things – even running water!

You will need:

Balloon

Balloon pump

1 Pump up the balloon. Stretch the neck and tie a knot in it, so that the air does not escape.

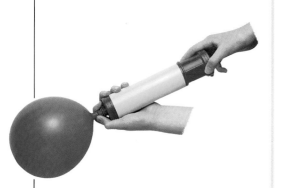

2 To give static electricity to the balloon, rub it.

Rub the balloon on something woollen, like a sweater.

3 Hold the balloon near running water from a faucet. The water bends toward the balloon!

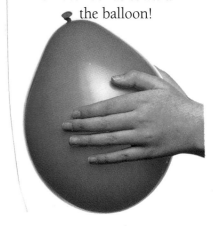

---

83 Make a propeller

Static electricity can repel objects as well as attract them. If you rub two pens they will repel each other, because they have both gained static electricity.

You will need:

Cotton thread

Two plastic pens

Silk scarf

1 Tie some thread around the middle of one of the pens. Position the thread so that the pen balances when it is dangled in the air.

2 Rub one end of each pen with a silk scarf. Dangle one pen from the thread and bring the two rubbed ends toward each other.

3 Static electricity pushes the pen around like a propeller!

84 Jump with electricity

Get some paper people jumping up and down! You can do this by using the static electricity you get when you rub a balloon. They jump both ways because static electricity can repel objects as well as attract them.

You will need:

Pen

Scissors   Balloon   Balloon pump   Stiff paper

1 Draw some small people on the paper.

2 Carefully cut them out. Make as many people as you like.

3 Place all your paper people on a tabletop.

4 Pump up the balloon until it is quite big. Tie a knot in its neck so no air escapes.

5 Rub the balloon on some woollen clothes.

Electric fields

Run a comb through your hair a few times and then see how it picks up bits of paper. An invisible electric field forms around an object as it gains static electricity. The comb's electric field reaches the bits of paper and attracts them so that they cling to it. For the same reason, a comb can also make your hair stand up.

6 Hold the balloon about 4 in (10 cm) above the people. They jump up and down!

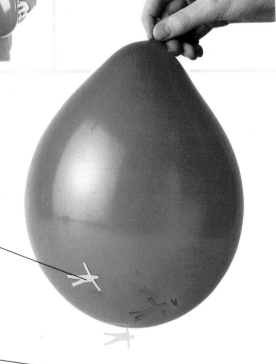

At first, the electricity in the balloon attracts the paper people.

After the people have stuck to the balloon, the static electricity repels them.

The people jump up and down again and again as they are attracted and repelled.

85 Wave a magic wand

Use the power of electricity to turn yourself into a magician. At the wave of a wand, you can make some little silver balls dance on a record! In fact, it is static electricity, not magic, that makes them dance for you.

You will need:

Sharp pencil

Glass or plastic bowl

Silver balls for cake decoration

LP record

Clean, dry handkerchief

1 Rub the record briskly with the handkerchief. It gains static electricity.

Use an old record that no one wants to play anymore.

2 Immediately, put the record on top of the bowl. Have the silver balls ready.

Some parts of the record have more static electricity and attract the balls.

3 Drop a few silver balls on the record. They roll about, and then suddenly stop.

Safe from lightning

A tall building often has a lightning conductor. This is a pointed rod that reaches from the top of the building to the ground. It can weaken the static electricity in the clouds, and this can prevent lightning from striking the building. If it does strike, the conductor leads it safely to the ground.

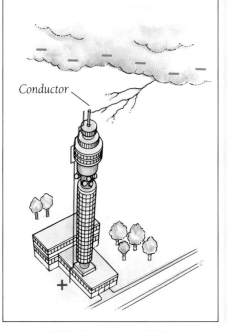

Conductor

The balls roll away to other parts of the record with more static electricity.

The electricity gets weaker where the pencil points.

4 Bring the pencil toward the record. As the point gets near each ball, it leaps away and dances around!

86 Build a charge detector

Rubbing an object such as a plastic comb or a balloon gives it a charge of electricity. Find out how to detect an electric charge – then see how the charge can move.

You will need:

| Long nail | Scissors | Plastic pen | Aluminum foil |

Round card | Thread | Plastic comb | Tape | Glass jar

1 👭 Ask an adult to push the nail about two-thirds of the way into the center of the card.

2 Tie the middle of a piece of thread tightly near the sharp end of the nail.

3 👭 Cut two strips of foil and tape them to the ends of the thread.

4 Place the card on the jar, with the foil strips hanging inside. Tape it in place.

Use only very small pieces of tape.

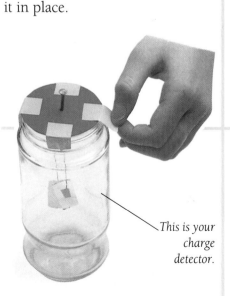

This is your charge detector.

5 Run the comb quickly through your hair several times.

Make sure your hair is dry.

6 Run the comb along the head of the nail. The foil strips move apart. This shows that the comb has an electric charge, which passes to the strips.

The charge travels down the nail and to the strips.

The charges on the strips repel each other.

The charge travels out of the strips and to your hand.

7 Touch the top of the nail. The strips collapse and hang down.

The electric charge cannot flow out through the plastic pen, so the strips keep their charge.

8 Charge the detector again. Now touch the nail with a plastic pen. The foil strips do not collapse.

Hair raiser
When you pull a sweater off you may see sparks. These are caused by static electric charges that leap between the sweater and your head.

87 Construct a circuit

Current electricity moves. When a battery is connected up properly, current electricity comes from one of its terminals. It then follows a path called a "circuit" back to the other one.

You will need:

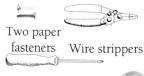

Two paper fasteners   Wire strippers

Screwdriver

Thick cardboard

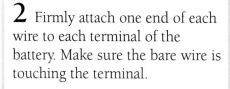

Coated wire   1.5V battery   1.5V bulb   Scissors   Bulb-holder

Steel paper clip

---

1 Cut two pieces of wire. Carefully strip away the plastic ends and then twist the bare strands of wire together.

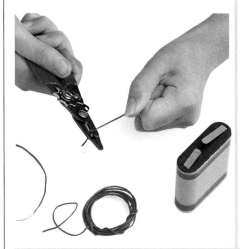

2 Firmly attach one end of each wire to each terminal of the battery. Make sure the bare wire is touching the terminal.

3 Make one wire touch the base of the bulb and the other one touch the side. This forms a circuit and the bulb lights up.

4 Screw the bulb into the bulb-holder. Attach the wires to the bulb-holder as the picture shows. The bulb lights up again.

5 Break the circuit by removing one of the wires from the battery. The bulb goes out because electricity cannot pass the gap.

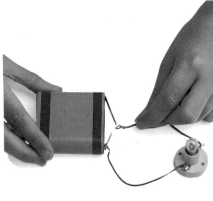

6 Cut a third piece of wire. Strip the ends and twist the strands of wire, in the same way as you did in step 1.

7 Fix one end of the third piece of wire to the battery terminal that is no longer connected.

8 Cut out a piece of card measuring 1 in (3 cm) by 2 in (5 cm). This is the base of a switch.

9 Wind the end of the wire from the bulb-holder around a paper fastener. Push it through the card.

10 Repeat step 9 with the wire from the battery. Put a paper clip around the paper fastener this time.

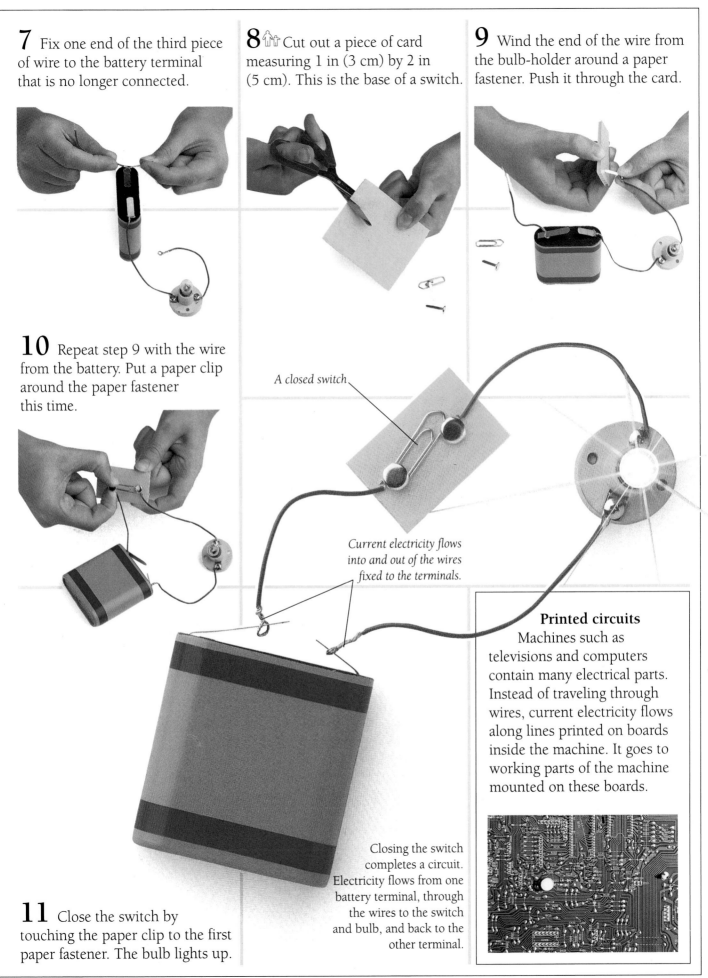

A closed switch

Current electricity flows into and out of the wires fixed to the terminals.

Closing the switch completes a circuit. Electricity flows from one battery terminal, through the wires to the switch and bulb, and back to the other terminal.

11 Close the switch by touching the paper clip to the first paper fastener. The bulb lights up.

Printed circuits
Machines such as televisions and computers contain many electrical parts. Instead of traveling through wires, current electricity flows along lines printed on boards inside the machine. It goes to working parts of the machine mounted on these boards.

88 Probe for electricity

Electricity does not flow through all materials. Wires that carry electricity are often coated with plastic to stop electricity from passing from the wire into other materials that it touches. Make a bug that shows if electricity can pass through something.

You will need:

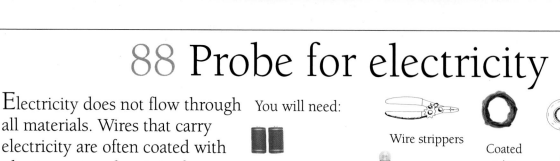

Two 1.5V batteries

Wire strippers

3.5V bulb

Coated wire

Three pipe cleaners

Tape

Colored card and paper

Aluminum foil

Sequins

Scissors

Bulb-holder

Glue

Screwdriver

1 Tape the top of one battery firmly to the base of the other, with a foil square between them.

2 Cut lengths of wire 10, 5, and 3 in (25, 12, and 8 cm) long. Tape the 10-in (25-cm) wire to one battery.

Strip the ends of the wires.

3 Connect the 5-in (12-cm) and 3-in (8-cm) wires to the holder. Tape the 3-in (8-cm) wire to the other battery.

5-in wire

Screw the bulb into the holder.

3-in wire

4 Tape the bulb-holder to the batteries. Roll paper around the batteries and wires to make a bug.

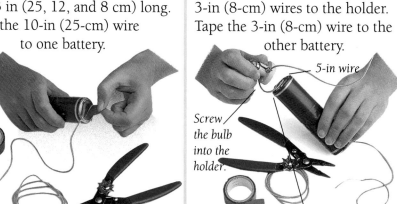

Make big eyes with ovals of card and sequins.

10-in wire attached to base of batteries

Make legs with pipe cleaners.

Tightly wrap the ends of the wires in balls of foil.

5 Touch the foil balls on the bug's feelers to different kinds of materials. The bulb lights up if electricity can pass through the material.

5-in wire attached to bulb-holder

Aluminum foil "conducts" or passes electricity. It completes a circuit so that the bulb lights.

89 Build a battery

A battery contains chemicals that it uses to make electricity. You can make your own simple battery with salt, foil, and coins. These contain the chemicals needed to produce electricity.

You will need:

Two wires with stripped ends

Six copper coins

 Tape

 Marker

 Saucer

Paper towels

Scissors

Aluminum foil

Warm salty water

Earphones

1  Draw and cut out six coin-sized foil circles and six paper ones.

2 Tape one wire to a coin, and the other wire to a foil circle.

3 Dip a paper circle in the warm salty water.

4 Put the foil circle with the wire in the saucer. Place the wet paper circle and a coin on top.

5 Build up more layers of foil, wet paper, and coins. The coin with the wire goes on top. This is your battery.

Inside a battery
This is a long-life battery that has been broken into pieces to show the materials inside it. Electricity comes from the terminals at the top and bottom of the battery.

Base of battery

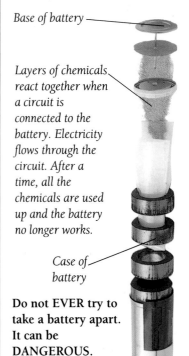

Layers of chemicals react together when a circuit is connected to the battery. Electricity flows through the circuit. After a time, all the chemicals are used up and the battery no longer works.

Case of battery

Do not EVER try to take a battery apart. It can be DANGEROUS.

Top of battery

6 Attach the end of one wire to the base of the plug of the earphones.

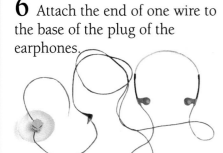

The electricity goes to the earphones and makes the sounds.

7 Put on the earphones. Scrape the end of the other wire on the tip of the plug. You hear crackles in the earphones!

When you place aluminum, salt, and copper together, they make electricity.

90 Make a merry-go-round

Electric motors power many modern machines. You can even buy a small one to work a merry-go-round. Electricity makes the shaft of the motor spin and drives the merry-go-round.

You will need:

Large and small rubber bands

Plastic tape

Modeling clay

Clear glue

Small cardboard box

Four thread spools

1.5V battery

Scissors

3 ft (1 m) covered wire

Colored paper

Knitting needle

1.5V–4V electric motor

Pencil

Wire strippers

24 pipe cleaners

Cotton swab

Switch
(see experiment 87)

Marker

Colored felt

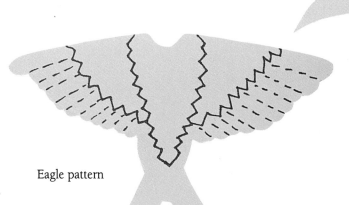

Eagle pattern

Swallow pattern

1 🖑 Cut three pieces of wire and strip the ends. Cut a piece of cotton swab and place it on the shaft of the motor.

2 Connect the three wires to the motor, battery, and switch as the picture shows. Glue the motor to the side of the box.

3 Roll a strip of paper around the knitting needle. Remove the strip and push it firmly into the center of one of the spools.

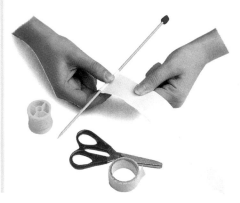

4 Glue the spool to the bottom of the box. Stick the other three spools to the knitting needle with clay as the picture shows.

5 Stretch the large rubber band around the box. Fit the small rubber band around the bottom spool on the needle.

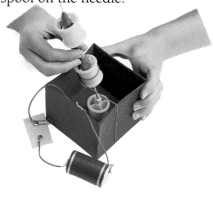

6 Make frames for six birds to sit on the merry-go-round. Use pipe cleaners to form the head, body and wings of each bird.

7 Trace the eagle and swallow patterns on felt. Cut out six bird shapes and tape them to the pipe-cleaner frames.

8 Using pipe cleaners and tape, attach the six birds to the top two spools. Push the knitting needle into the spool in the box.

9 Stretch the small rubber band so that it fits over the piece of cotton swab on the shaft of the electric motor.

10 Press the switch, and the birds spin around! Electricity from the battery turns the shaft of the motor. This moves the rubber band, which turns the knitting needle.

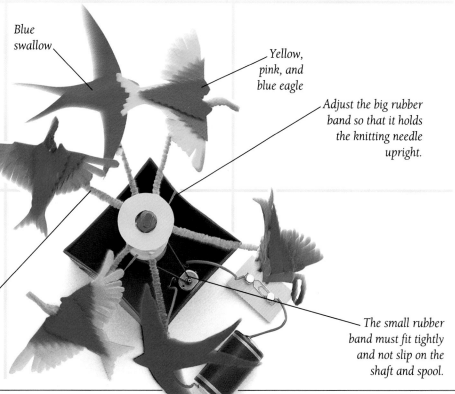

Blue swallow

Yellow, pink, and blue eagle

Adjust the big rubber band so that it holds the knitting needle upright.

Pink and blue eagle

Pipe cleaner supports

The small rubber band must fit tightly and not slip on the shaft and spool.

107

MOTION AND MACHINES

The world around you is on the move. People and animals walk, run, swim, and fly. The wind blows, rivers flow. Machines are on the move, too, performing tasks for people. A machine, like everything that moves, works because a force pushes or pulls it. The force can come from a powerful engine or motor – or just human muscle.

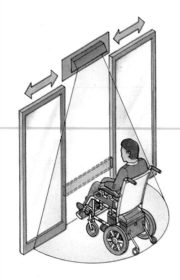

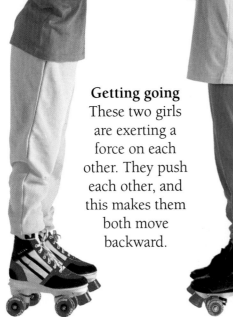

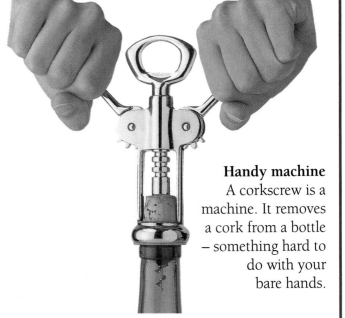

Good opening
Automatic doors work themselves. They send out invisible rays. These detect movement so the doors open as people approach.

Quick thinking
A calculator is a machine that does math equations for you. It works at lightning speed.

Perfect performer
A robot is a very advanced kind of machine. It can be instructed to carry out complicated tasks, and it does them perfectly.

Getting going
These two girls are exerting a force on each other. They push each other, and this makes them both move backward.

Handy machine
A corkscrew is a machine. It removes a cork from a bottle – something hard to do with your bare hands.

108

91 Build a wheelbarrow

Machines can give you more strength! Build your own wheelbarrow and move a heavy load of stones. The wheelbarrow is a "lever" – a machine that can increase the force you use to move things.

You will need:

 Plastic bag

 Short pencil

Thread spool

Tape

 Small stones

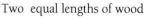 Two equal lengths of wood

Card

Shoe box

Scissors

1 Put the stones in the bag and lift them. You need to exert a lot of force.

2 👥 Cut the card to the same width as the box. Tape the card inside to make two sections.

3 Tape the lengths of wood firmly to the bottom of the box.

4 Stick the pencil through the spool. Tape the pencil to the ends of lengths of wood.

5 Put the bag of stones in the back of the barrow. Try lifting it.

It is easier to lift the stones when they are in the barrow.

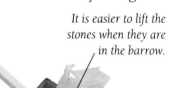

The lengths of wood form a lever that tilts around the wheel.

You need less effort when the load is nearer the wheel.

The spool is the wheel of the barrow. It must turn easily.

When you use a lever, your hands move farther than the distance the load moves. This extra movement gives the lever the extra force to lift the load.

6 Move the bag of stones to the front of the barrow. Now it is very easy to lift the heavy load.

92 Get a jet going

Airliners fly around the world at high speed. They have large jet engines that produce a powerful jet of air to drive the airliner through the sky. Show how a jet engine works by flying a balloon at speed across a room.

You will need:

Length of thread

Sticky tape Balloon Balloon pump

Drinking straw

1 Feed the thread through the straw. It must move easily.

2 Stretch the thread across a room. Stick two pieces of tape to the straw.

Make sure the thread is tight.

No air must escape from the balloon.

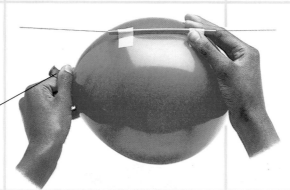

3 Blow up the balloon. Hold the neck, and attach the balloon to the straw.

A jet of air leaves the neck and pushes the balloon forwards.

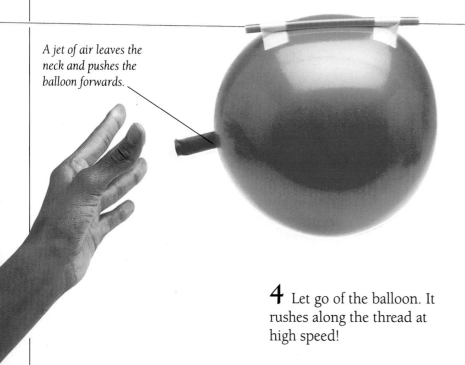

4 Let go of the balloon. It rushes along the thread at high speed!

A fast move

Jet engines power the fastest cars in the world as well as high-speed aircraft. A jet engine sucks in air at the front and heats this air with burning fuel. It then sends the hot air blasting out from the back of the engine. This forces the aircraft or car forward at very high speeds.

93 Build a turbine

A turbine is an engine powered by a moving liquid or a gas. You can build your own turbine out of straws and power it with the air from your lungs!

You will need:

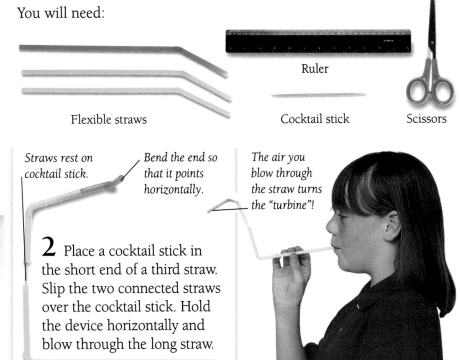

Flexible straws

Ruler

Cocktail stick

Scissors

1 ✂ Cut the long ends off two flexible straws, about 1.5 in (4 cm) from the bend. Push one straw end into the other.

Straws rest on cocktail stick.

Bend the end so that it points horizontally.

2 Place a cocktail stick in the short end of a third straw. Slip the two connected straws over the cocktail stick. Hold the device horizontally and blow through the long straw.

The air you blow through the straw turns the "turbine"!

---

94 Test for friction

It's much easier to slide on something smooth, such as ice, than on a rough surface. This is because rough surfaces create more friction than smooth ones, and friction slows things down.

You will need:

Screwdriver

Thumbtacks

Knife

Pen

Wood block

Hinge and screws

Protractor

Ruler

Quarter circle of card

Two lengths of wood

Test surfaces such as felt, sandpaper, and card

1 ✂ Screw the hinge to the two lengths of wood. Now one length can lie flat while the other slopes.

2 Using the protractor and ruler, draw a scale of angles on the card. Fix this to the bottom length of wood with the thumbtacks. Place a test surface on the top length of wood.

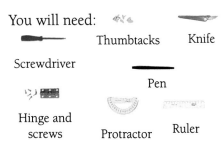

3 Place the block on the end of the surface. Tilt it until the block starts to slide. The angle shows how much friction the surface creates.

You can use oil or water to reduce friction.

The steeper the slope, the greater the friction.

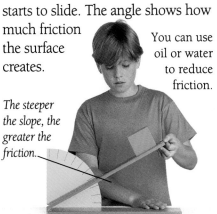

95 Move in a circle

A special kind of force is needed to make something move in a circle. It is called "centripetal" force. See how this force keeps an object moving in a circle instead of flying off.

You will need:

Wood block with a hole in it

Thread spool

Cork

String

Drill and bit

1 Drill a hole through the center of the cork. Tie a big knot in one end of the string and thread the other end through the cork and the spool.

2 Tie the other end of the string to the block. Check that the string runs easily through the thread spool and that the knot keeps the cork from coming off the string.

3 Hold the thread spool. Move it so that the cork whirls around. The block rises as the cork circles around the spool.

The cork tries to fly outward.

The weight of the block holds the cork back. This weight is the centripetal force.

96 Engage gear

Gears are pairs of wheels which link so that one turns another. Gears of different sizes turn at different speeds, and make it possible for machines to change speed. Try making some gears of your own.

You will need:

Two nails

Glue

Thread spools

Assorted jar lids

Thick card

Sandpaper

1  Glue sandpaper strips around the edges of the lids. Glue on the spools as shown.

2 Push nails through the card. These are axles for your gear wheels.

3 Place a different-sized wheel on each nail, so that they touch. Turn them, using a spool as a handle.

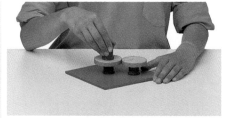

97 Make an automatic machine

Machines often need people to operate them in order to work properly. But some need no one to control them. This automatic machine sorts big marbles from small ones, all on its own!

You will need:

Straw

Kebab stick

Scissors

Glue

Tape

Long cardboard box

Two short cardboard boxes

Modeling clay

Large and small pieces of card

Big and small marbles

1 👫 Cut openings in the long box and in one of the short boxes. The picture shows where these should be. Glue the short box to the top of the long box.

Two openings

Two openings

2 Fold the small piece of card lengthways to make a chute. Use pieces of clay to attach it to the top of the other small box.

Small piece of clay

3 Make channels in the large piece of card by folding the sides. Tape a straw underneath and insert the stick.

Folds

4 Stick two small marbles to one of the channels with clay. Place the stick on two blocks of clay, so the weighted side touches the table.

5 Line up the boxes, the chute, and the card, as the picture shows. Roll a small marble down the chute.

The small marble rolls into the upper box.

Small marbles

Big marbles are heavy enough to tilt the card, but small marbles are not.

Big marbles

Mail machine
Letters and parcels go through automatic sorting machines. These can detect zip codes marked on the mail, and sort letters and packages going to different towns into different compartments.

6 Roll a big marble down the chute. The card drops, and the marble goes into the lower box.

98 Construct a fan

Keep cool – with a hand-powered fan. This machine uses a belt that works in the same way as a gear. It makes the fan spin faster than the handle that you turn to make it work. Many machines have parts like these that work together at different speeds.

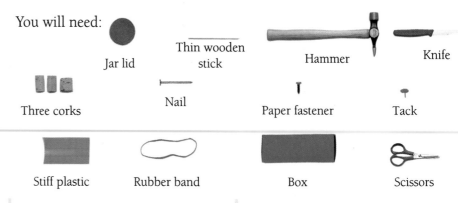

You will need:

Jar lid

Thin wooden stick

Hammer

Knife

Three corks

Nail

Paper fastener

Tack

Stiff plastic

Rubber band

Box

Scissors

1 👫 Ask an adult to make two holes in the front of the box, and another in the back, opposite one of the first holes. Ask the adult also to make two holes in the jar lid, using the nail.

Put the holes 2 in (5 cm) from the top and bottom of the box.

Make one hole in the middle of the lid and the other near the edge.

2 👫 Using the tack, attach a cork to the jar lid. This is the handle of your fan.

Push the fastener through the lid and the second hole in the box. The handle should turn easily.

3 Attach the handle to the box with the paper fastener.

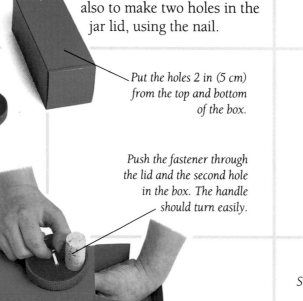

Slant the slits.

4 👫 Ask an adult to cut four evenly spaced slits in another cork. Now two corks are in use.

5 👫 Cut four long strips from the plastic. Make them as wide as the slits in the cork.

6 Push the plastic strips into the slits, and push one end of the stick into the cork.

7 Push the stick through the other two holes in the box. The stick should poke out from the back of the box.

Push the stick right through the box.

8 Push the third cork onto the end of the stick. Loop the rubber band around this cork and the handle. Your fan is now ready.

The rubber band should fit without much stretching.

The rubber band is a belt that links two wheels: the lid and the cork.

Riding at speed

The chain on a bicycle is a belt that causes the back wheel to turn faster than the pedals. When you change gear, the chain moves from one of the gear wheels on the hub to another. The size of the gear wheels affects the speed at which the back wheel turns. Smaller wheels make the bicycle go faster.

9 Turn the handle of the fan. The blades spin rapidly and blow air forward!

The blades spin faster than the handle turns.

The jar lid is a bigger wheel than the cork. This causes the cork to turn faster than the lid.

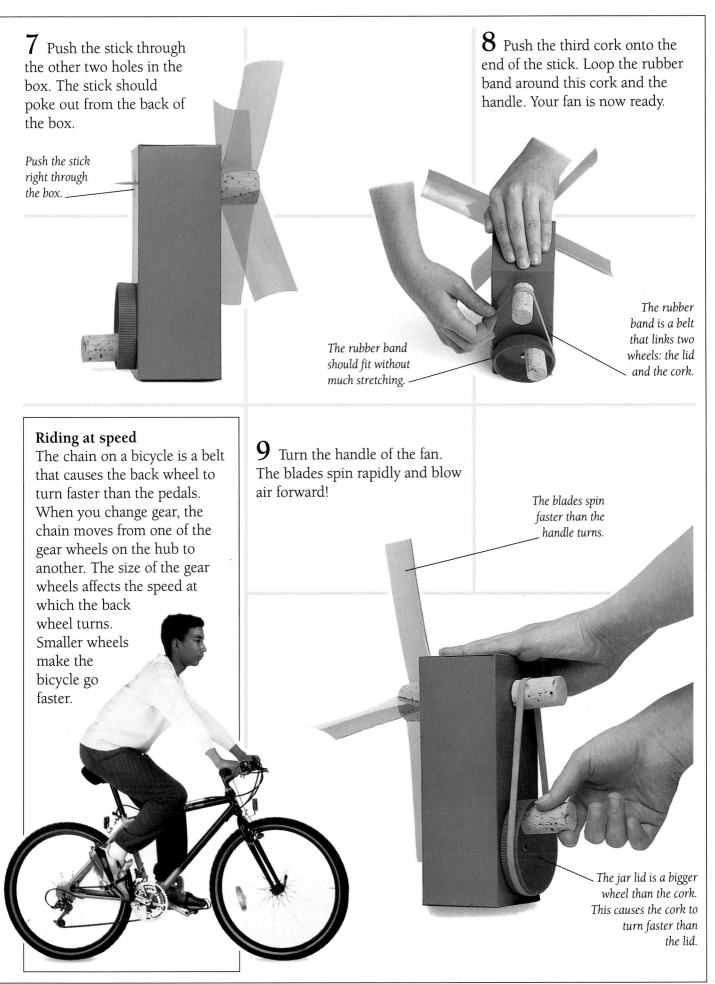

115

99 Build a water wheel

Many machines have a motor or an engine to produce the force they need to make them move. The first kind of motor or engine was the water wheel. It uses the power of flowing or falling water to drive a machine. Water wheels are still used today.

You will need:

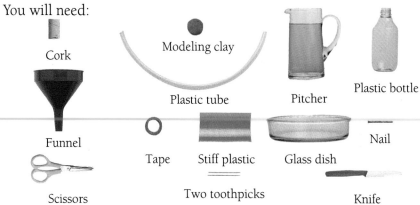

Cork

Modeling clay

Plastic tube

Pitcher

Plastic bottle

Funnel

Tape

Stiff plastic

Glass dish

Nail

Scissors

Two toothpicks

Knife

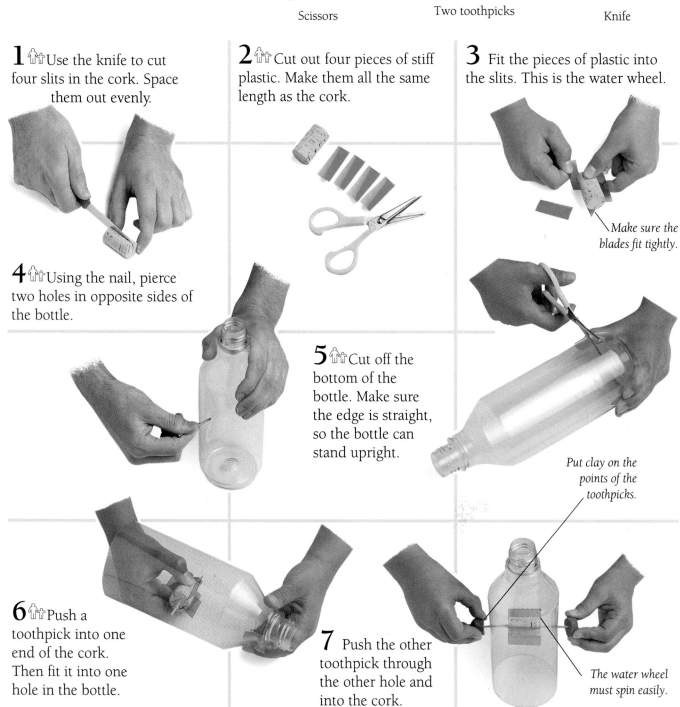

1 Use the knife to cut four slits in the cork. Space them out evenly.

2 Cut out four pieces of stiff plastic. Make them all the same length as the cork.

3 Fit the pieces of plastic into the slits. This is the water wheel.

Make sure the blades fit tightly.

4 Using the nail, pierce two holes in opposite sides of the bottle.

5 Cut off the bottom of the bottle. Make sure the edge is straight, so the bottle can stand upright.

Put clay on the points of the toothpicks.

6 Push a toothpick into one end of the cork. Then fit it into one hole in the bottle.

7 Push the other toothpick through the other hole and into the cork.

The water wheel must spin easily.

8 Push the funnel into one end of the piece of plastic tube. Wind tape around the funnel and tube to hold them firmly together.

Ask a friend to pour water into the funnel.

9 Place the bottle in the dish. Fit the tube into the neck of the bottle. Pour water into the funnel, and the water wheel spins around.

Direct the stream of water to hit the plastic blades of the wheel.

Hold the funnel and the tube.

The water moves faster because it is falling a greater distance.

In a hydroelectric power station, water falling down a pipe from a dam spins the blades of a turbine in the same way as this water wheel. The turbine drives a generator that makes electricity.

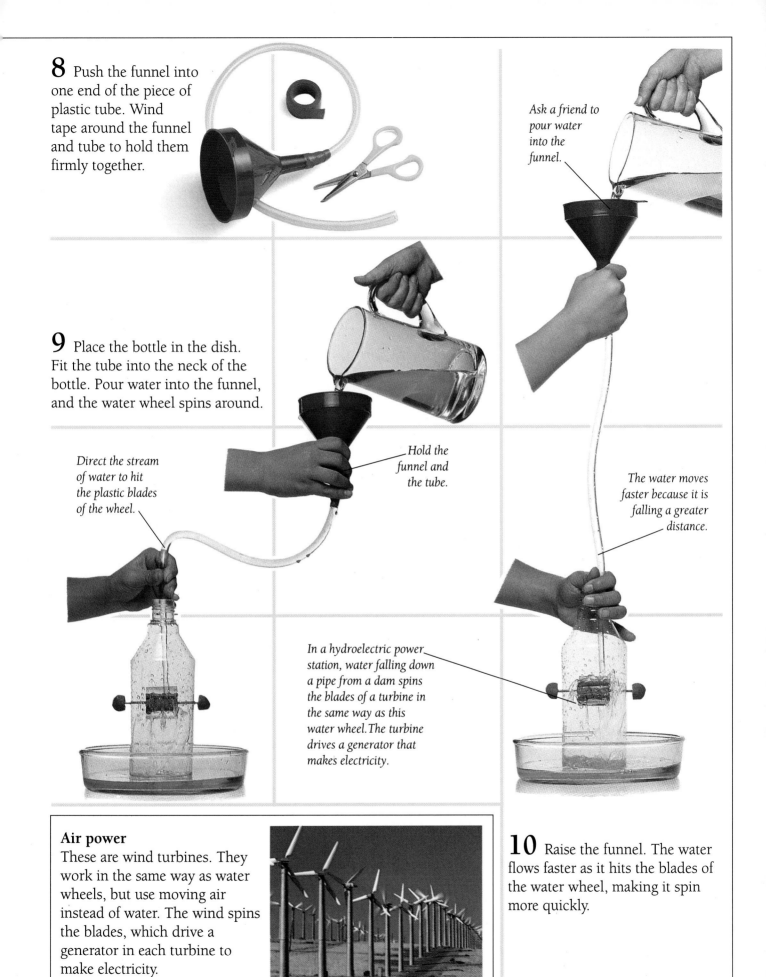

Air power
These are wind turbines. They work in the same way as water wheels, but use moving air instead of water. The wind spins the blades, which drive a generator in each turbine to make electricity.

10 Raise the funnel. The water flows faster as it hits the blades of the water wheel, making it spin more quickly.

100 Lift a load with water

Raise a heavy weight – with just a little water! Using water in this way is called "hydraulics." Very powerful machines that lift, push, or press things work by hydraulics. It greatly increases the force that they produce.

You will need:

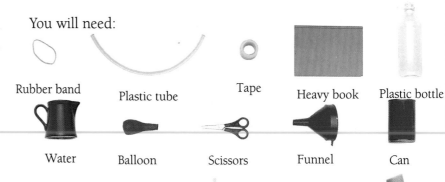

Rubber band   Plastic tube   Tape   Heavy book   Plastic bottle

Water   Balloon   Scissors   Funnel   Can

1 Fit the neck of the balloon over the end of the tube. Seal it tightly with tape.

2 👫 Cut the top off the bottle. Make a hole in the side, near the base of the bottle.

3 Push the balloon through the hole in the side of the bottle.

4 Tape the funnel firmly to the other end of the tube, as the picture shows.

5 Place the can inside the bottle, on top of the balloon. Then lay the heavy book on the bottle.

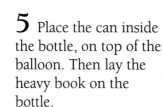

Big digger
Powerful excavators like the one in this picture use hydraulics. Pipes carry a liquid from a pump to cylinders, where the liquid pushes out pistons with great force. The pistons drive the bucket into the ground and raise a heavy load of soil.

6 Lift the funnel and pour some water into it. The balloon slowly swells – and lifts the heavy book!

The swelling balloon exerts enough pressure to push the heavy book upwards.

Raise the funnel above the book.

The weight of the water in the tube pushes water into the balloon.

101 Build a crane

A crane is able to lift a heavy load high in the air. It has a wheel called a "pulley" to produce a lifting force, while a "counterweight" keeps the crane from tipping over as it lifts a heavy weight.

Tape   Paper clip   Pen top   String   Hammer   Scissors   Marbles

Length of wood

Strong cardboard box   Plastic cup   Two nails   Two thread spools   Heavy book

1 Nail one spool to the end of the wood and nail the other spool near the other end.

Make sure the spools can turn easily.

2 Cut a hole in the box. Insert the wood so that it sticks out at an angle.

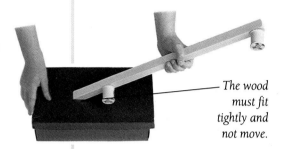

The wood must fit tightly and not move.

3 Cut a short piece of string. Tape it to the cup to make a handle.

4 Push the pen top into the lower spool. Tape one end of the rest of the string to this spool.

5 Loop the string over the upper spool. Hold the end firmly and wind the string onto the lower spool.

The pen top is your handle.

6 Bend the paper clip to make a hook. Tie it to the end of the piece of string.

The upper spool is a pulley wheel. It changes the downward force of the handle into an upward force that lifts the load.

7 Place the book on the box. Fill the cup with marbles and hook it to the crane. Wind the handle to lift the load of marbles.

The book is a counterweight. Its weight prevents the weight of the load from pulling the crane over.

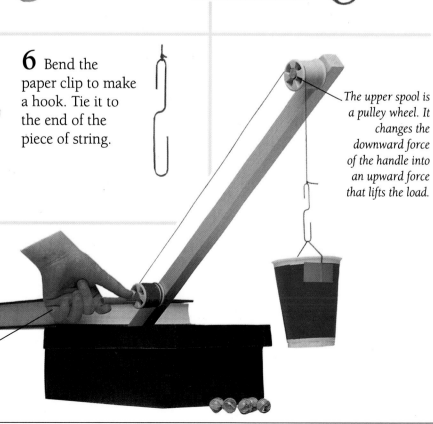

Index

Acknowledgments

DK Publishing would like to thank:
Andrea Needham, Nicola Webb and
Tracey White for design assistance.
Andy Crawford, Jane Burton, Michael
Dunning, Pete Gardner, Frank
Greenaway, Colin Keates, Dave King,
Ray Moller, Stephen Oliver, Gary
Ombler, Tim Ridley, Clive Streeter
and Kim Taylor for the commissioned
photography. Models Kirsty Burns
and Paul Cannings.

Picture credits

t=top b=bottom c=center l=left
r=right
Allsport 9b, 110 br.
Ardea / John Daniels 86br.
Catherine Ashmore 85br.
Bruce Coleman / Alain Compost 66bc.
Robert Harding Picture Library 18bl,
76bl / Photri 70bl.
ICI Paints 51bl.
Image Bank 16cr, 31b, 48tl, 59br,
96tl, 113bc, 117bc / Andre Gallant
34bc / Jean-Pierre Pieuchet 16tl / Al
Satterwhite 118bl / Weinberg / Clark
48tr.
Lupe Cuhna Photo Library / Vaughan
Melzer 66tl.
Jonathan Metcalf 50br.
NHPA 24b / Trureo Nakamuta 74bl.
Royal Navy Submarine Museum 39br.
Perskke Price Service Organisation
57tr.
Planet Earth Pictures 23 bl.
David Redfern Photography 66tr.
Rockwater 88br.
Science Photo Library 25bl, 57bc,
79bl / Ron Church 19bc / European
Space Agency 16cl / Jack Finch 86tr /
Simon Fraser 103br / Peter Ryan /
SCRIPPS 20bc.
Spectrum Colour Library 61bl.
The Stockmarket 45br.
Tony Stone Worldwide / David
Austen 28tr.
Survival Anglia 58tl.
Thrust Cars Ltd 110br.
Zefa 9bl, 16tr, 96bl / Harlicek 33bc /
H. Lutticke 35bc.